CDevelopment Tools for the IBM PC

Al Stevens

A Brady Book
Published by Prentice Hall Press
New York, New York 10023

C Development Tools for the IBM PC

A Brady Book
Published by Prentice Hall Press
A Division of Simon & Schuster, Inc.
Gulf+Western Building
1 Gulf+Western Plaza
New York, New York 10023

PRENTICE HALL PRESS is a trademark of Simon & Schuster, Inc.

Manufactured in the United States of America

2 3 4 5 6 7 8 9 10

Library of Congress Cataloging-in-Publication Data
Stevens, Al, 1940–
    C development tools for the IBM PC.
    Includes index.
    1. C (Computer program language) 2. IBM Personal
Computer—Programming. I. Title.
QA76.73.C15S73 1986   005.265   85-16660

ISBN 0-89303-612-9

Limits of Liability and Disclaimer of Warranty

The author(s) and publisher of this book have used their best efforts in preparing this book and the programs contained in it. These efforts include the development, research, and testing of the theories and programs to determine their effectiveness. The author(s) and publisher make no warranty of any kind, expressed or implied, with regard to these programs or the documentation contained in this book. The author(s) and publisher shall not be liable in any event for incidental or consequential damages in connection with, or arising out of, the furnishing, performance, or use of these programs.

Registered Trademarks

About the Author

AL STEVENS has been a computer programmer and systems analyst for more than 27 years. His programming career has spanned several generations of computers, from those with vacuum tube logic to the recent personal computer. For the last seven years, Al has been an independent consultant with clients in business, industry, and government. He helps his clients with requirements analyses, proposals, software specifications, and data base design, but he prefers programming. He began using the C programming language in 1982 and now regards it as "the ideal language for the professional programmer."

When he isn't writing software, Al actively pursues interests in music, art, and airplanes. He has been employed at various times as a newspaper cartoonist, a jazz pianist, a dixieland cornet player, and an automobile mechanic.

This is his first book.

Foreword

This book has reusable C language software tools that directly support the development of on-line, interactive. software systems. The tools are developed to run on an IBM PC, XT, or AT, but, since the code is written to minimize the few portability problems associated with C, other implementations are possible.

The collection includes file management, indexed data management using B-trees, executive menu management, screen forms management, and the sorting of data, either from file to file or as an in-line function to a program. This book is unique because it provides these capabilities to you, the programmer, in source code form with no royalties or other strings attached. Many examples throughout this book use these tools, and a discussion of the underlying principles applied in their development is included.

These software tools are not mere textbook examples. They are genuine, functioning software modules in use in many real applications around the country. I wrote the programs for use in a software consulting practice. The book came later in reaction to the interest expressed by colleagues and clients in the toolset and its use.

Acknowledgments

Thanks are due to Ron Herold and Pat Thursam who helped me by critiquing early versions of the manuscript. I also wish to express my gratitude to Ted Byrne who made significant contributions to the content and style of the work. A word of thanks goes to Terry Anderson for his guidance and supervision. And special thanks is for Judy Stevens, my wife, friend (and companion). She helped with the editing and logistics, and she was patient.

About the Source Code

The software in this book is used in a wide number of systems in the installations of my clients. Here is a list of some applications where the toolset functions are in use.

1. A data base administrator's package that manages the data element dictionary and data descriptions for a relational data base.
2. A government procurement and contracts financial management system.
3. A multiuser system simulator.
4. The membership and catalog processing for a video tape rental store.
5. A C language cross reference utility package.
6. A government architect and engineering bid specification text management system.
7. A facilities design and construction project management system.

The source code in Appendix A is available to anyone. You can key it in from the listings in Appendix A, or you may prefer to purchase it on an IBM PC-compatible double-sided diskette by mail order. Send $25.00 to:

C Software Toolset
2983 Newfound Harbor Drive
Merritt Island, FL 32952

(Florida residents please add 6% sales tax.)

Contents

Preface

We are currently experiencing a phenomenon that has come to be known as the "information explosion," a condition where the availability and demand for information exceeds our ability to process it. This circumstance has been nurtured and fed by the remarkably wide proliferation of small, inexpensive computers; as the potential for information processing has grown, its demand has also grown.

The growth in demand for processed information has spawned a parallel phenomenon called the "software crunch," meaning a shortage of information-processing software. Not enough expensive software is available to feed the inexpensive hardware, and there are not enough programmers to develop it.

This shortage of programs and programmers can be dealt with in two ways: by increasing the number of programmers who are producing code, and by improving the productivity of the ones we already have. The first approach involves the school system. University computer science departments are grinding out graduates as fast as they can, and there is no problem replacing them with new, eager freshmen. The second solution, improving the productivity of the individual programmer, is necessary regardless of how many there are and is the reason the software in this book was developed. Tomorrow's programmer must be more productive than today's.

A lot has been written on the subject of programmer productivity and how to improve it. Most of the research addresses itself to either the problems of managing software projects or the methods and techniques of software design and development. Both views are valid, and both have been seriously examined and expanded upon during the past two decades. Unfortunately, we have yet to correct the dilemma which is characterized by this wry observation found tacked above programmers' desks:

"Good, fast, cheap—select two."

The sad fact is that when we select two, there is no assurance of a successful outcome; often we cannot get even one out of the three.

Disciplined software development is clearly understood and taught today, but too often large projects ignore the advanced methods developed from years of research and experience. In this book, I will explain those methods that influenced the development of my software tool collection. By example, you will be urged to accept the practices of structured programming, information hiding and, most of all, software tool building. If you do not already know what these things are, then you will learn and not a day too soon.

This book identifies the components of interactive computer applications common among many systems. Applying the disciplines just named I developed those components in a way that will allow them to be reuseable. This constitutes a personal collection of software tools, one that allows a programmer to be more productive. The quantity of code required for a given program is proportionately reduced by the size and scope of the applicable tools from the toolset. The less code you need to write, the more programs you can complete.

This book, then, has four purposes:

1. To promote the use of software tools in the development of interactive systems.
2. To provide a healthy starter set of useful tools for the C programmer.
3. To set an example of orderly and disciplined design and development practices, characterized by reusable tools and the disciplines of structured programming, portability, and information hiding.
4. To provide the reader with motivation and materials to become a more productive programmer.

This is most appropriate on the eve of an era when the attribute of productivity, more than any other, will mark the difference between success and failure in the profession.

Al Stevens

1

Introduction

This is a book about C language software tools for interactive systems. Interactive systems are systems where a user interacts with the computer to process some information. This book includes C source code for many of the functions common to this environment. It does not try to teach you how to program or how C works; there are other texts for those purposes. It will, however, try to influence your thoughts about programming and style. This book is intended to fill a void that the author has encountered during the development of software systems.

Who is the audience for this book? You are a programmer who will be writing programs for on-line users in an interactive environment. You need to understand the fundamentals of data storage and retrieval and the requirements for data entry and display, and you need a set of software tools that helps you apply that understanding to the creation of interactive software systems.

I begin to fill those needs with this software. At the same time I introduce several algorithms that you might not have seen in source code before, and I set the examples of structured programming and software tool building.

The software tools in this book run on the IBM Personal Computer, but these principles are applicable in other environments. The functions compile and execute by using the Aztec C86 Compiler, the De Smet C Compiler, and the Lattice C Compiler. These compilers are accurate implementations of "standard" C. That is, they implement most of the language as defined by Kernighan and Ritchie in "The C Programming Language." All three compilers come with a nearly complete standard library of functions. This standard library lets us develop code that has a better chance to be portable—to be moved from system to system.

Some Definitions

In these discussions, we define the person who uses the software you develop as the "user." The "user interface" is the dialogue between the computer and the user. An "application" is the user's use for the system, as in a personnel or payroll application. A software function that calls another function is called the "caller" or the "calling program or function." A "function" is a module of C source code, as in the idiom of the language. A "process," as used here, is a generic use of the computer system within the application, such as the generation of a report.

The Tools

Many software components are common to most on-line, interactive systems. In this book, I specifically address a certain category of application (discussed later). These components are alike enough in their implementations that they can be supported by using a common set of software functions. Let's identify and explain the components. They are:

Menu Management
Data Screen Management
B-Tree Index Management
File Record Management
Record Buffer Management
Sorting

A full set of software functions that adequately supports these components is the beginning of a good software development tool collection. In this book I develop a C programmer's toolset through the use of reusable C language functions.

Figure 1-1 is the system architecture for a software system developed around the C tool functions. The shaded box represents the applications functions; the rest of the boxes are toolset functions. The figure shows the top-down relationships of each of the sets of functions. A function is called by those above it and calls those below it; the cylinders are disk files and the arrows show the direction of data. Suppose that the shaded box is a set of functions to support the interactive processes of membership accounting for an association or a club. If the system is not very complex, there might be 500 lines of code. The rest of the system is handled by the several thousand lines of code from the C software toolset. The advantages of a tool collection are becoming obvious.

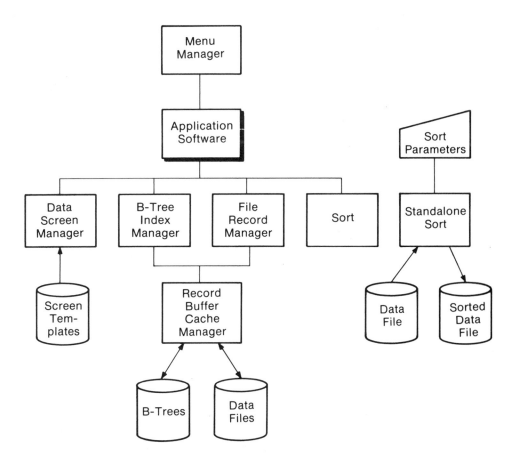

Figure 1-1. C tool functions: system architecture.

Menu Management

Traditional interactive computer systems use menus to allow the user to control the execution of programs. Recently, wonderful machines like the Macintosh have emerged with things called "icons" and hardware "mice" to improve the user-machine interface. These are some great concepts, but the software in this book is not aimed at these techniques. Not yet, anyway. The large majority of today's systems, and, I would guess, the large majority of those to be sold for the next several years are going to use the old-fashioned keyboard and screen. That is the environment supported by the software in this book. That environment uses menus.

Data Screen Management

Most on-line systems communicate with the user by using the video screen, and the user communicates with the system by using the keyboard. <u>The terminal is the medium</u>. In the typical personal computer BASIC program a lot of PRINT and INPUT statements manage this dialogue. These statements represent system prompts and user-entered data items in response to those prompts. It is my goal to replace this BASIC programming technique with a toolset of C functions for controlling the user interface in a consistent manner. The objective is to eliminate a lot of redundant programming and achieve a measure of consistency in the user interface. A library of such functions can be used again and again, thereby reducing the programming effort required for the development of subsequent applications. This is the strength and the common sense of software tool building.

The system developer describes screen formats and provides data collection buffers, and the functions do the rest. Well, almost. Exit points must be provided for the functions to call custom code which does those jobs that are specific to a particular application—special data validation, help to the user, record retrieval, and so on.

B-Tree Index Management

Interactive systems access on-line data from a random access storage device such as a hard disk. To be interactive, this access needs to be fast. It needs to be fast enough that the user doesn't suffer undue delay. Therefore, the computer system must be able to locate a record of data from anywhere in perhaps tens of thousands of records and retrieve it and do something meaningful with it in a very short time. The retrieval is based on some descriptive data entered by the user. For example, a personnel system user may wish to locate the record of a single employee based upon the employee number. There are a lot of techniques for doing this; different environments can be supported with different techniques. In the interactive environment the records in a file must be located by using various data items at different times. The employee might be located by employee number for one retrieval, by social security number in a different retrieval, by last name in a third, or by department in another. This requires a technique where files can be searched by using the values of more than one data item and where some item values are known to uniquely identify a record (a given employee number is in only one employee file record), while others can be shared by multiple records (the same department number can appear in more than one employee record). The data item used for the search is called a "key." A data item, which is the primary identification for a record (for example, the employee number in the employee file record), is called the "primary" key. A nonprimary key data item that can also be used to search a file (for example, the department number in the employee file record) is called the "secondary" key. Usually, the primary key is unique in a file, and secondary keys can have multiple occurrences of the same value.

A common technique for supporting a data file with multiple keys is the use of inverted indices. An inverted index is another file that is a table of the data item values and is maintained separate from the data file itself. It contains an entry for each value of the data item in the data file and a pointer to the data file record that contains the value. When searched, the index yields the file record address of the relevant data record. The search must be efficient; if there are a lot of entries in the index, its structure must support some technique for rapidly finding a desired entry. The index itself must be maintained. That is, if a data record is added, the index must be updated with an entry to point to the new record. When a record is deleted, the index entry that points to it must also be deleted. When a record is modified, and the change is to an indexed item, the old entry in the index must be deleted, and the new one must be added. To achieve an interactive environment, these index maintenance operations must be fast.

There is a technique for inverted index table maintenance called the B-tree. This is a hierarchical structure of balanced (hence "B-") indices which has the property of providing fast key retrieval and updates. It is maintained external to the data structure of the file it supports, so it can be eliminated or built at any time without affecting the integrity of the data itself. The tree structure of the index allows a particular entry to be found with a minimal number of key value comparisons. It has the additional capability of providing instant sequential access to the file using the indexed data item. This sequencing can be in ascending or descending order and can start from any record in the file. This often eliminates the need for data file sorting; a given file can be processed as though it were in any of several sequences without the need for an intervening sort pass. This saves a lot of time for on-line retrievals of ordered data.

B-trees are very popular among the developers of data base management system software packages. The B-tree structure has the fascinating ability to appear maintenance-free. Older methods of inverted indexing always seemed to require periodic rebalancing or reorganizing of the indices to maintain efficiency. The B-tree grows and subsides by itself and rarely needs tending.

There must be software functions to build, maintain, and retrieve keys from B-trees. Therefore, this book includes a complete set of B-tree inverted index functions. With these, our toolset expands, as does our understanding of advanced data structures. The B-tree functions represent a significant and complex piece of code. The technique itself is popular; books are available that explain it in-depth, and software packages are available that implement it, but the source code is rarely made available.

File Record Management

When a data record is stored on a disk, it must be written in a location that is known to be available (not already in use) and that can be remembered later when the record is to be read back in. Operating system file managers will allocate physical disk space to a file and provide a directory that allows an application program to find it. Programming languages provide the interface between the application software and the operating system to open and close files and to read and write records. It is the responsibility of the programmer to manage the functional integrity of the data in the records.

The software in this book provides for the description of a file of fixed length records of any size and the random storage and retrieval of a record based upon the record number relative to its location in the file. The first record will be known as record 1, the second as record 2, and so on.

Using these toolset file record management functions, you can retrieve and replace existing records and add new ones. You can also delete existing records. Usually a system that allows the deletion of random records leaves an empty space in the file where the record was located. It would be better if the empty space formerly occupied by a since deleted record could be reused for a new record. Therefore, the file record management software keeps track of deleted record positions and reassigns the space when new records are to be added.

Record Buffer Management

When record access is random and the file is big or there are several files, disk access can be slow. The seek time is significant, and the mechanical action of the disk drive is often noisy. This is not to suggest that we abandon random access; it is certainly faster than serial access when a particular record is required from within the depths of a big file. Many system manufacturers have provided a buffering scheme that reads and writes blocks of sectors to and from memory. Then, memory transfers are performed in response to read and write requests. This is very effective for files that are accessed serially in the physical sequence in which the records were written. However, it has no advantage when the records are accessed in a random pattern, unless a very large number of buffers is allocated.

The software tools in this book include a miniature cache memory subsystem to be used for random access files. Cache memory is a technique where the data in a slower device (disk) are "cached" in a faster device (random access memory or "RAM"). It is a particularly effective method when the file has records that are accessed frequently and others that are not.

Caching is used by the B-tree index manager and the file record manager. If you use these packages, you probably won't find any other need for the cache, but the calling conventions are provided later in the book so that you can understand their use.

Sorting

The B-tree functions allow a file to be accessed in one of several predefined sequences. The sequence is represented by an inverted B-tree index. But what about those occasions when a required sequence is not represented by one of the indices? The file must be sorted into a different sequence. Usually this involves creating a new file of data in a different physical sequence. Often the file is used for a report or query response and does not need to survive beyond the creation of the desired output. The tool collection includes a sort program that can be called from an applications program. It also features a stand-alone sort program that can be used for file sorting. The popular Quicksort algorithm is used along with a system of sort work files and a binary merge. The technique is fully described in Chapter 10.

Why This Tool Collection?

There are software packages available that do some of what these tools do. Why don't we use them? Often that is a viable solution and you can use many of these packages quite effectively. But they do not always support everything you want to do. Usually you find yourself modifying the requirements of the application to mold it to the package because the source code of the package is not available for you to modify. This is the tail wagging the dog. Many times dog-wagging is an economical approach, but, just as often, it represents a reluctant compromise. The strength of the tool-building concept is in its flexibility. A compromise is not necessary because the tools in this book are under your control. You can add to them, you can make new tools out of old ones, and you can choose which ones to use for each unique situation.

Many of the commercially available, general purpose programs are oriented to an environment where the user is situated "at the computer" doing "personal computer things." The user is cognizant of the computer environment. The user is "computer-literate." There are modes to be toggled in and out, control key sequences to be aware of, and, generally, a lot of computer cognizance to keep up with. Users who have other concerns need support at a level that allows them to concentrate on matters outside of the computer while still using it. We tend to forget that our users are not programmers, and that they don't think like us. They don't want to think like us; some of them don't even like us. A user once told me, "We're people, not programmers!"

Consider this example. In a point-of-sale situation (a retail store with a cash-register-like terminal), the salesperson's attention should be on the customer and the product rather than on the computer. The user interface should encourage this rather than impede it.

There are other reasons for using these tools. Packages tend to be available for a family of computers. It is usual to find a package that only runs on an Apple, or on an IBM PC, or, more generally, on a CP/M or MS-DOS computer. If you develop your application around such a package, then it is not portable. That is, it cannot be moved to a different family of computers unless you redevelop it to be compatible with the new family.

A prime advantage of the C programming language is that software developed with it can be portable. You can move the source code to another computer where there is a C compiler, and, if you write portable code, the programs should compile and run in the new environment with a minimum of modification. But, if your software is based on the use of a package, and you don't have the source code, you are out of luck. It isn't portable. You can't move the package to the new configuration. With the tool collection you have all of the source code written in good old portable C, and it doesn't use any nonstandard functions unless it includes the source.

A later chapter addresses the problems of portability and what I ran into when I moved these functions around. Portability is an objective. You don't find out what kind of code is nonportable until you try to move it, when your good intentions can leave your breakfast on your face.

If you have gotten this far, you must have an interest in the software toolset concept. Strive for portability, and strive for a set of reusable, portable tools. Take them with you to a new job. You might find yourself to be the most productive programmer in a team of grizzled veterans because you don't need to rewrite every low-level function every time you want to solve a new problem.

The User Environment

What is the best application for this particular toolset? We are concerned here with a certain kind of interactive user environment. This software does not solve every problem. You will not find much help in writing arcade games, interactive graphics, or word processing software. Those are all interactive systems. There is more than one kind of interactive user. Who is ours? First, let's look at what a user really is.

The distinction between "operator" and "user" has dimmed over the years. In the old days, the operator ran the computer, while the user coded data entry sheets and received reports. The operator knew little about the applications, and the user knew less about computers. This is frequently still the case for large systems, but today's general trend is towards small, interactive systems where the user is also the operator. Operating the computer is not the user's primary function. However, using the computer is a part of the user's job, and that involves operating it. So, we define our user as a person who has job-related concerns other than the computer, but the computer is an integral part of the user's daily activities.

This software was installed in a rental operation that maintains records of inventory and clients, product movement, and many other uninteresting things. The user is the store operator.

I started to install one of the popular packages that the personal computer software industry calls a "data base management system" or DBMS. DBMS is a term that was redefined by the fledgling PC industry. In the world of bigger systems, it meant a system with a host of features not offered in most of the typical personal computer data base packages. Even without the features, these packages are generally quite good and can do a lot. Besides, they are cheap. However, my voyage into these small system file handlers (what they really are) showed me that there are too many deficiencies in them for my user. For example, I need to have several related files on line at one time. Most of the packages are one or two file systems. To have multiple files with the packages, you must define multiple "data bases" and access them individually, in a nonrelated fashion. Further, I need to build custom data validation routines that are executed at the time the data elements are entered. Most packages provide for data entry on a screen, and limited validation of the data after all of the data has been entered.

That option simply is not acceptable. The user needs to enter a rental transaction as it occurs without paying a great deal of attention to the computer. Then, if the customer has an expired membership, or has an overdue item, or some other exception occurs, I want the computer to immediately report the exception. That is what "interactive" is all about. Without custom entry points (called the "host language interface" in the big time) and interfile relationships (a true data base management system), I cannot build the kinds of data entry routines that properly support the user.

All this and more reinforces the conviction that a set of software tools is needed that allows the development of serious software systems to do what I want them to do. If the tools won't allow that, then I can modify the tools. To that end, the software in this book was developed. These tools are published so that others like me can get on with the business of making computers work for them.

The C Language

The selection of C as the basis for our software tool collection was the result of the natural compatibility between the objectives of the problem and the characteristics of the C language environment. C includes features that make it particularly applicable to the task of software tool development. It is a portable, concise, and extensible language.

The portability of C is its best known attribute because of its use in the development of UNIX, the portable operating system. Portability is a controversial issue, and the problems encountered when moving these tools around are discussed at length later in the book. I have learned from this experience that C is not as portable as is often thought, but that it is the most portable of the many languages I have used. Further, my discussions with other programmers about their use of other near-portable languages lead me to believe that C is the most portable of them all. These discussions can tend to become emotional and riddled with high-strung opinions (including my own), so I encourage you to develop your own ideas on the matter.

The concise nature of C is what endears it to the professional programmer. It is difficult to categorize, because it looks like a high-level language, yet it has a lot of the advantages (and pitfalls) of assembly language. It also allows the use of some very elegant syntactic expressions which deliver extremely efficient object code.

You don't often hear C described as an extensible language. The terse nature of its syntax and its ability to accept new data type definitions are what make it so. C is a language of functions. There are not many "verbs" in C. The complete list of C verbs is `goto`, `return`, `break`, `continue`, `do` and `switch`.

The verb `goto` is rarely used, `return` is used to terminate a function, and the rest support structured programming's control structures (see Chapter 2 for a discussion of this). So, in effect, there are no real verbs in the language as we would think of them in, say, COBOL.

A C program consists mainly of control structures (`if`, `while`, and so on.), assignments, expressions, and function calls. You extend the language by adding functions to implement new verbs. The standard library function "strcpy" (string copy) is an example of an extension and can be thought of as a loose equivalent to the COBOL MOVE verb. There might be some resistance to the notion that functions in C can be compared to COBOL verbs, but consider these from the standard function library: `open`, `close`, `read`, and `write`. These words are verbs. (By the way, they are also COBOL verbs.)

The Hardware

The functions in our tool collection operate in the Personal Computer environment. They have been ported to a number of different configurations, and the code published in this book is the IBM PC version, which has been compiled by using the De-Smet, Lattice, and Aztec C compilers. Usually only the screen and keyboard drivers (terminal.c as described in Chapter 5) need to be rewritten when the software is moved to other hardware. There are no fixed assumptions about the configuration of the screen, although the display-centering algorithms in the menu functions need to be considered when your screen is other than 24 lines by 80 columns. There are global symbols to change these and other hardware-related differences. These are discussed in the various chapters of the book where they are related, and they are summarized in the discussion of portability found in Appendix B.

Reading List

Here is a list of books you might use for reference material while you explore this book. Some of them are about C, others contain discussions of the concepts and algorithms that are implemented in the functions in this book.

—"The C Programming Language," Brian W. Kernighan and Dennis M. Ritchie, Prentice-Hall.

—"Programming in C," Stephen G. Kochan, Hayden Book Company.

—"The C Programmer's Handbook," Thom Hogan, Brady Communications Company, Inc.

—"Design of Man-Computer Dialogues," James Martin, Prentice-Hall.

—"Fundamentals of Data Structures," Ellis Horowitz and Sartaj Sahni, Computer Science Press, Inc.

—"The Art of Computer Programming, Volume 3, Sorting and Searching," Donald E Knuth, Addison-Wesley Publishing Company.

—"Software Tools," B. W. Kernighan and P. J. Plaugher, Addison-Wesley Publishing Company.

—"Reliable Software through Composite Design," Glenford J. Myers, Van Rostrand Reinhold Company.

Conclusion

With the introduction of the software tool collection concept, we have established some objectives and goals for ourselves. By the time we are through building these tools, we will be able to design and implement interactive systems in C that are portable, durable, maintainable, consistent, easy to use, and effective in their support of the user. Our programming skills will be sharpened through the use of tool building, and our productivity will be improved by the use of the software tools developed in this book. Later as our personal tool collection grows, this productivity will continue to grow and broaden.

The chapters that follow describe software functions to do the things we have discussed here. The functions are written in C and are intended to be used in a software system that is also written in C. The reader is encouraged to carry these concepts as far as the imagination allows.

2

Software Development Philosophy

This chapter discusses the practices that were used in the development of the software toolset in this book. No system of this size can (or, at least, should) be developed without some kind of strategy for software development and implementation. These toolset functions are building blocks. They do not stand alone, so they cannot be developed in secrecy, to be used by programmers who have no knowledge of the underlying principles of their development. They are a personal collection of tools for anyone who uses them. If there are lessons to be learned from the experience of developing the software in this book, then those lessons must be shared. You need to understand your tools.

This software was developed by using certain programming disciplines and objectives. Sometimes the objectives were met, and sometimes they were not. Occasionally the disciplines were relaxed, but not without good reason. Here are the principles that were applied in the development of this software.

- The functions were developed to be portable.
- The programs were designed "top–down" and developed "bottom-up."
- The software was written with structured programming techniques.
- The software uses the concept of "information hiding" where data and structures not relevant to a function are not seen by its code, and the code of a function does not rely on data or structures that are not related to its purpose.

- The software is the framework for a comprehensive software toolkit. It consists of reusable tools each of which can be used alone or in integrated combinations with the others.

I encourage you to read these discussions even if some of the details seem abstruse at first. You will want to return to this when you begin to implement the code.

Portability

C is portable. That is, a program written in C can be run on any computer having a C compiler. At least, that's what they tell us. It is almost true. The language enjoys a widely accepted standard, and most compilers strive to implement that standard. The standard C definition is given by Kernighan and Ritchie in "The C Programming Language." This definition is so widely recognized that a simple reference to "K & R" in any discussion of C is instantly understood and acknowledged by all aware participants.

If compilers are developed with a standard language definition, then programs written in the language should compile successfully on different computers. There are several reasons why this doesn't always happen. Here are some of them.

Coding Practices

The C language promotes the development of portable code, but it does not enforce the practice. For example, knowing that the integer size on a compiler is 2 bytes, you can offset through a data structure by using a constant 2 to get past integers. This works until a compiler with a different integer size is used. C provides a vehicle (sizeof) to avoid this kind of nonportability, but cannot force its use. The standard for the C language could demand that all implementations adhere to a common integer size, but then the efficiency of the compiled code would be affected, and the original C language objective of tight, efficient executable code would be compromised.

Similarly, most of the following obstacles to portable code can be overcome with conscientious and disciplined coding practices.

Hardware Differences

Differences exist between computer hardware architectures that influence how a compiler is written. An example is in the order of assignment of characters to memory words. Some computers with

2-byte words put the first character in the least significant byte of a word and the second character in the most significant byte. In storage, the string "SOFTWARE" appears as "OSTFAWER." Other computers store strings in the sequence in which they are defined. You are not normally aware of this while doing character and string operations, but if one of the character pairs is treated as a computer memory word rather than as 2 bytes, the difference is going to be a problem when you port the code to the opposite environment.

Certain computers impose variable boundary alignment requirements on the compiler. For example, the integer might need to start on an even-numbered byte. If there are structures containing strings and integers, the compiler will insert padding wherever it is needed to keep the integers aligned properly. Other machines may not need automatic alignment, so the resulting structure compiles to different lengths on those different machines. Once again, it would have been possible for the language standard to have specified alignment rules, but then there would have been an undesired performance compromise.

If either the string in the first example or the structure in the second example is part of an external data file, the software might be portable while the data files are not. The data must be converted before the software operates properly.

The Standard

The C language standard is not specific about some critical considerations. For example, the order in which function arguments are evaluated is not specified. I suspect that this is because the Kernighan and Ritchie standard was written after several differing compilers were already in use. It is possible to write a function call with side effects and get different results from different compilers. This is an acknowledged ambiguity, and you are encouraged to write code that avoids it. Consider this line of code:

```
fn (t [i], i++);
```

As written, the code gives the opportunity for the result to depend upon the direction of the evaluation of the statement. The array is subscripted by the variable i with its original value in some compilers, while other compilers compute the subscript after incrementing i. It is better to make your intentions clear by using unambiguious code. A better (and portable) way of coding the previous statement is:

```
fn (t [i], i);
i++;
```

Often the absence of explicit specification in the standard language definition causes a de facto standard to emerge, usually based on the UNIX implementation of C. (The language originated with the development of UNIX, so it is natural that the UNIX version of the compiler would be used as the baseline.) Other times, there is equal distribution among the compilers of the possible interpretations of an ambiguity.

Compiler Differences

Different compilers (even for the same machine) can exhibit different characteristics. The dissimilarities can be small, but the implications can be significant. Sometimes these dissimilarities are the result of interpretation of the standard, and often they are long-standing and tolerated discrepancies. In Appendix B, I discuss some of the differences between compilers used for the IBM PC.

Compilers differ on the number of characters that are significant in variable and function names. This value commonly varies from six to eight characters of significance and is often influenced by the assembler and linking programs supplied with the operating system. Assemblers convert the assembly language output from the C compiler into relocatable object files. The linker is used to construct an executable program from one or more of those object modules. Either program can impose a limit on the number of significant characters in an identifier. Some compilers provide their own assemblers and linkers. Kernighan and Ritchie say, "No more than the first eight characters are significant, although more may be used." They then go on to explain that external identifier names for functions and external variables are implementation dependent.

Standard Library Differences

The widest differences between compilers can be found in their implementation of the standard C library. C is a language of functions. The language itself provides no facility for file management, string handling, input/output or other operating system interfaces. All of these aspects of a computer program must be implemented through a function library. As a result, a standard library of input/output, memory allocation, data conversion, string processing and mathematical functions has evolved. The names, parameters and calling sequences of these functions are widely known, and the standard is accepted by the users of the language. However, the implementation of the library into different compilers seems to involve some measure of interpretation by those doing the implementing. It is as if they want to improve the standard. Recently, there has been a gradual shift toward standard library compliance as newer versions of popular compilers are released. This trend is a good one and will foster the growth of portable code as an objective in itself.

Operating System Differences

Some functions in the standard library cannot be implemented in some environments because the operating system does not support the requirements of the functions. MS-DOS does not include the concept of a user identification, so the standard library functions **getuid**, **getgid**, **geteuid**, **getegid**, **setuid** and **setgid** cannot be supported. Programs using these functions cannot be ported to MS-DOS without modification. In another example, CP/M-80 does not include a calendar and clock, so the functions dealing with time cannot be implemented under that operating system.

The operating system can also influence how a function might process. The UNIX convention for the **argc** and **argv** parameters (Kernighan and Ritchie, p. 110) in the **main** function of a program specifies that the name of the executed program is pointed to by **argv** [0]. CP/M and MS-DOS cannot deliver this, so the compiler writer must decide decide just what **argv** [0] does point to.

In another example, the end-of-file convention differs among operating systems. The various compilers treat the matter differently. Since the UNIX file system always remembers where the last character in a file is located, the standard library read functions can sense end-of-file when an access goes past that character position. The MS-DOS and CP/M-80 operating systems only remember the location of the last sector, so the different compilers deal with the problem differently. What happens at end-of-file is different in different compilers.

Function Names

Suppose there is a function in the system named "my_function." Everything works as it should, and the software is ported to a different compiler. For some reason, unseen parts of the internal system begin to misbehave. When you debug, you find that my_function is executing at unexpected times. If the source code for the compiler's library is available, you might learn that this new compiler has its own function called my_function. Because the application's relocatable object modules are linked ahead of the compiler's library, all of the library functions' calls to my_function are resolved by the application version of it, rather than the compiler's version of it. Many linker programs will resolve like named functions with the first one encountered without giving any warning indications. The obvious solution is to rename the application function. But, the real problem is in the diagnosis of the situation. It can take a good amount of digging to discover that the new compiler has its own my_function. Identification of the problem is made more difficult when the compiler's function is an internal one, not documented and not meant to be called from software other than its own library functions.

Often, systems functions are prefixed with an underscore character as the developers try to avoid this problem by making their function names unique. Of course, this convention loses its advantage as you mix a lot of different systems software packages. Some compilers will allow the dollar sign to be used in function names. The notion is that only special, hidden functions will use it. This, however, is not a widely adapted practice and will certainly result in nonportable code.

Compiler Enhancements

Most C compilers deliver a language system that includes a UNIX-like standard library of functions. The idea is to look as much like UNIX as possible. A good compiler tries to get the standard functions implemented as close to the UNIX baseline as possible. This collection of standard library functions plays a significant role in the promotion of C as a portable language. But then, there are the enhancements. Everyone has additional functions that go beyond the standard, and their use is tempting. But, beware: Use them and portability is endangered.

One of the major deficiencies in the C language (in my opinion) is in its treatment of structures and members. The K&R standard specifies that a named member can appear in more than one structure only if it has the same variable type in both structures and if the offset to the member is the same in all structures (that is the deficiency). This limits the use of a common identifier for the same data item when it appears in many structures. Why, even COBOL allows that! In fact, it is dangerous to use a common identifer in several structures; a later modification to the data formats could cause a lot of code to require modification. The Lattice C compiler has corrected the deficiency. But, take advantage of their contribution to the technology, and your code is no longer portable.

Currently an American National Standards Institute (ANSI) standard for C is being considered by the Institute's X3-J11 committee. This standard, if accepted, will allow for nonunique member names and will correct for the deficiencies. Once the standard is published, most compiler vendors will probably comply with it.

Additions to the Standard

The C language has changed with time, and all of the changes have been improvements. The void function type, the enumerated data type, and structure assignment are three of the additions to the language. Unfortunately, not all of the compilers support the new features. If you use them, the code cannot be ported to a compiler that does not implement them.

There is a temptation to assert that we will simply avoid nonstandard compilers and only associate with the best and latest. If you have the luxury of that position, then, by all means, stick with it. In reality, we are often assigned to the environment at hand, and it to us, and the choice is not ours to make.

Top–Down Design

When the ideas for these functions were orginally developed, there was a picture in mind very much like that shown in Figure 2-1. That was the original design. It isn't much, is it? But, it represents the germ of an idea—the top level of a design for a software toolset. The natural next step was the development of a list of areas that the functions would support. The list eventually became the overview that can be seen in Figure 1-1. Figures 2-1 and 1-1 are the first components of a top–down software design, so called because the design begins with a view of the system at the highest level and then progresses downward. Each successive lower level views the software in more detail.

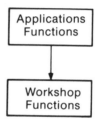

Figure 2-1.

The overview in Figure 1-1 shows the "subsystems" of the tool collection. The next step is to describe each subsystem in terms of its component parts. The specific functional processes to be performed by the subsystem for the application are defined. For example, the B-tree index management subsystem decomposes into the component parts shown in Figure 2-2.

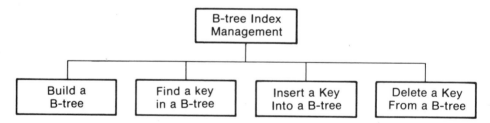

Figure 2-2. Component parts of the B-tree index management subsystem.

In fact, after you get underway, several other things need to be provided; but, initially, this chart is the second level view of the B-tree subsystem. Every other part must be similarly decomposed.

Later, I will discuss the concepts of B-trees with nodes and keys and all of the functions to support them. For now, since this is a discussion of the top–down design concept, it is only necessary to know that a B-tree is a hierarchy of records called "nodes" each one containing a list of indexed values called "keys."

The decomposition of a component of a subsystem involves breaking it down into lower level components. The result is a chart showing the hierarchy of processing that supports the component. This chart is often called the "structure chart." Figure 2-3 is a structure chart for the function that finds an indexed key value in a B-tree.

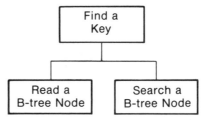

Figure 2-3. Structure chart used to find an indexed key value in a B-tree.

This structure chart shows that the function that finds keys must execute two other functions, one to read a node, and one to search a node. The purpose of a structure chart is to show the relationship of the functions, but it does not express program logic. It identifies the functions to be developed and shows which functions call which other functions.

The decomposition may continue downward; lower-level structure charts are developed at each step. Or it may stop at any level when it arrives at the lowest level of a software design. This lowest level is the "algorithm" that is to be coded into a software module. An algorithm is a formula or procedure that can be coded into a software function.

After reaching that point, the next step involves the design of the algorithms. There is a preferred technique called "pseudocode." This is a high-level meta-language used to express the logic of an algorithm in a form similar to structured program code, but with natural language constructs to describe the procedural components of the algorithm. Pseudocode is independent of the development hardware and language environments. Figure 2-4 is a pseudocode description of the algorithm to find a key in a B-tree index.

In a formal system design project you might be required to deliver pseudocode or some other expression of the logic of the software. Older techniques, such as flow charts, might be used, but the pseudocode method is preferred by many designers because it presents the logic of the algorithm in a form that is already structured. This structured form encourages the programmer to write structured code.

```
/*--  This procedure searches a b-tree starting at the root node for an index
value which matches the argument x. If a match is found, the procedure returns
"true," the node number where the value was found and the location of the value
in the node. If no match is found, the procedure returns "false" and the node
number and location into which the value x may be inserted.  ---*/

/* node contents:  a[0], k/a[1], k/a[2],. . .,k/a[n] ,
   a = address pointers, k = key values */

procedure find__key (x)
     p = root node
     q = 0                          /* q will be the parent of p */
     while p > 0
          k[0] = 0, k[n+1] = infinity
          read node p
          search node p for k[i] <= x < k[i+1]
          if k[i] == x
               return true, p, i
          q = p
          p = a[i]
     return false, q, i
```

Figure 2-4. Pseudocode.

The pseudocode in Figure 2-4 includes an essential piece of software design documentation—the logic narrative, shown at the beginning of the code. This documentation is the English statement of the intention and processing of the algorithm and is often carried forward into the code as comments. Remember though, the value of a commented program is compromised if the code is changed and the comments are not. False comments can deliver a false sense of understanding to the reader and can cause otherwise good code to become unmaintainable.

Bottom–Up Development

We could take several approaches in the development of a system of software once the design is complete. The two techniques considered for the development of these functions are top–down and bottom–up. Other approaches that were rejected include helter-skelter (the sequence of development caters to developer whimsy), biggest function first/last, most interesting function first/last, and the "necessity-is-the-mother-of-invention" school of development, where you code functions only as the need for them looms imminent.

In top–down development, modules are coded and tested in the same sequence in which they were designed. The highest level module is worked on, then modules at the next lower level are developed, and so on, until, at the lowest level, all the modules are operational. This method has its advantages and its drawbacks. One major advantage is that when the designer is finished with a particular level of the design, the programmer can begin work without waiting for the full design to be completed. A disadvantage is that the functions below the level where coding is underway are not available; they haven't been coded yet. Therefore, they must be simulated. Usually, this process involves the development of "stub" programs that act in the absence of the missing functions by simulating their purpose. Often the stubs are null functions that either return a constant value or simply return. Most programmers, when faced with the development of lower stubs, go ahead and code the real thing, preferring that to coding stubs and keeping track of what has been stubbed and what hasn't.

In bottom–up development, the functions are developed at the lowest level first. Each function is tested by using higher stubs— programs that test the function by passing controlled constant parameters and displaying the results. For some reason, the use of stubs at a higher level is not perceived as a disadvantage.

Developing functions this way has a psychological advantage. Programmers think of each function to be developed as a unit of work that has a time of completion associated with it. When a function is declared to be operational following a bottom–up development, that task can be said to be over. There is nothing pending that can cause some of the work to be revisited. There are no lower-level functions yet to be developed, upon which the current function depends. We are not placed in suspense, waiting for some later development.

Most of the software in this book was developed by using the bottom–up approach as much for practical reasons as for any other. This book presents primarily a library of lower-level functions. The bottom–up approach, therefore, seemed more natural, since there is no real top to the code itself. Take another look at Figure 2-1. The top is found in the applications software that the functions are to support.

The Design and Development Environment

A design and development task involves two aspects that can influence the success of the project. While not the domain of this book, they are worth mentioning now. These two unrelated subjects can, together or individually, spell success or failure for a software development effort. They are:

- The requirements definition
- Haste

For any system, there needs to be a clear, unambiguous statement of the functional and performance requirements. This statement needs to be formally documented and agreed upon. The system should then be designed to support those requirements. If you do not have this definition, then I will guarantee that there will be unknown, unspoken differences of opinion about what the system is going to do, and you will not learn about them until the system is in use. The users, the designers, and the developers will all have different concepts. This results in poor support for the users, undeserved criticism for the developers, and a bad reputation for the computer. Without clearly defined requirements, you never know when you are finished.

The second factor that can compromise the quality of a software system is haste. This chapter discusses software development disciplines that require conscious application. They are always perceived to be expendable when the pressure gets turned on. The deadline looms, the short cuts abound, the disciplines are abandoned, and the system suffers. I never know what to do about this, because everyone agrees that it is expedient and, therefore, appropriate, "just this once."

Structured Programming

The software tools in Appendix A were developed by using most of the basics of structured programming. There are exceptions to this practice, and there are reasons for them. First let's consider what is meant by "structured programming."

The concept of structured programming has its foundation in the theory that any algorithm, no matter how complex, can be expressed by using only three programming control structures. These are:

- sequence
- if-then-else
- do while

The "sequence" control structure is used for operations where events in a program occur sequentially like this:

event 1
event 2
event 3

The "if-then-else" allows events to occur as a result of the test of a condition as in this example:

```
if condition then
    events
else
    events
```

The "do while" control structure provides for the iterative execution of events as long as a tested condition remains true. In the following example, the events occur if the condition is true; otherwise they do not. After each occurrence of the events, the condition is tested again. If it is still true, the events occur again. This procedure is called "looping."

```
while condition do
    events
```

The evolution of structured programming revealed that a program that uses only these three control structures can be read beginning at the first statement and continuing downward to the last. What's more, the program would be written without the use of the "go-to" statement. Generally, these practices lead to code that is easier to read and, therefore, easier to maintain. Subsequently, the industry discovered that structured programs are also easier to write.

This research led to the definition of a "proper" program. In the view of structured programming advocates, a program is proper if it uses one entry and exit, the control structures of structured programming, no infinite loops, no unreachable code, and no go-to statements.

Since the original research, additions have been made to the three control structures. Even though any program can be written with just the original three, the additions have been developed and accepted because they retain the original spirit of structured programming. They are convenient, and there are frequent occasions where their use is preferred over one of the other three. These control structures are:

    until
    for
    case

"Until" is similar to "do while" except that it causes at least one iteration of the events, and the iterations continue until the condition is true rather than while it is true. The structure looks like this:

    do events
      until condition

"For" provides for the iteration of events with the automatic modification of a variable and a condition that terminates the iterations.

    for variable = value1 to value2 by value3
      events

The variable is initialized with value1 and compared to value2. If they are not the same, the events occur and the variable is modified by value3. Then the loop repeats.

"Case" is a convenient way to execute one of a series of events based upon the value of an expression. It is often used as a substitute for if-then-else when a large number of conditions are to be tested and the conditions are all based upon a common expression.

```
case expression
    value
        events
    value
        events
    value
        events
```

The C language contains all of these control structures, although some of them have a slightly different appearance than the examples just given. The examples are intended to address the subject of structured programming at-large rather than just the C language. Here are the C language equivalent statements:

- "Do while" is in C without the word "do."
- "If-then-else" appears in C just as in the examples without the word "then."
- "Until" is represented by the C construct: do statement while (!expression); (The ! means "not.")
- "For" is more powerful in C than in most languages. It allows for any initializing statement, any iterating statement, and any terminating test. The three do not need to be related, and any of them can be a null statement or multiple statements.
- "Case" is represented in C by the switch operation. The word "case" is used where our example above uses "value."

C offers several extensions to the structured programming control structures. Among these are "break" and "continue". These statements allow the orderly interruption of events that are executing inside of loops. Also included is the much-maligned "goto" statement. Nearly every language designer includes the goto along with an apology for it, the advice that it should be avoided, some example of where it might be remotely appropriate, and the assurance that the language designers themselves never use it.

A Structured Tool Collection

It can be said, without reservation, that the programs in our toolset were developed by using structured programming practices. The code can be read from top to bottom, there are no "goto" statements or unreachable code and the accepted control structures are used. Therefore, the programs are structured. It cannot be said, however, that they all comply with the definition of "proper" programs. They are not "proper" for two reasons:

- Sometimes there are what appear to be infinite loops.
- Although every function has only one entry point, many functions have several exits (returns).

Occasionally, the following kind of code is seen in the functions:

```
while (TRUE)          {
    <statements>
    if <condition>
        break;
    <statements>
}
```

The "while (TRUE)" constitutes an infinite loop. The only way out of the loop is by execution of a "break," "goto" or "return" statement or through the use of a function that never returns (for example, execl, exit.) A more "proper" structure would be:

```
while (!condition)      {
    <statements>
    if (!condition)     {
        <statements>
    }
}
```

In cases where this approach makes for more readable code, it is used. However, when the proper approach causes the nesting and, therefore, the indentation of the source code to become very deep, I opt for readability over propriety.

The same reason allows the rationalization of the return of a function from places other than the end of a function. Remember, we are trying to write efficient and readable code as well as proper code. If the logic is several nested levels deep inside of a function and at a place where the function needs to exit with a value to return, there are few qualms about issuing the return statement right on the spot. To comply with the definition of a proper program requires the code to somehow get to the bottom of the function with the return value intact. Usually this means the use of a contrived variable used as a switch whose sole purpose is to guarantee that the code is proper. First, I don't like manufactured data elements. Second, it might not be obvious to the reader of the code why one is being used. The purpose of a return statement is always clear.

These departures from the definition of proper code are common in C programs. Most books on C (including K & R) have "improper" programs as examples. Don't get hung up on propriety; it doesn't prove correctness all by itself.

However, with respect to structure, I know this to be true: it is easier to write structured code; it is easier to read structured code; it is easier to maintain structured code; and, oddly enough, I am not sure I care to remember how to write code any other way, no matter what the language.

This zeal is not dogmatic. It demonstrates a simple preference, although a strong one. If you write unstructured code and it works, then perhaps your success should not be questioned. A suggestion that you review the practice and give the other side a try is not, however, out of line. The 4000 plus lines of structured code in Appendix A should prove that it is actually possible to develop large software systems without violating structure. Younger programmers do not generally need this counsel; the schools are teaching structured programming as the only natural way to write software. They even teach structured COBOL. Rather, these comments are aimed at those of my generation who are still practicing their craft with the older techniques. Possibly, some crafty readers will peer into Appendix A and ferret a hidden shred of poor structure, a remnant of early influences. Rather that than they should find a bug.

Good structure by itself does not constitute a good program. Using the recursive properties of C, you can code function calls into the same kind of incomprehensible rat's nest that unbridled goto programming will produce. Don't be lulled into a smug and false sense of confidence just because you leave out the goto statement.

A program can be structured (and proper), do what it is required to do, and still be a poor example of code. The first three common measures of good software are its reliability, maintainability, and extensibility. A reliable program is one that seldom fails. Given that most programs will occasionally fail, a maintainable program is one that is easy to fix. An extensible program is one that can be modified when the requirements change.

These are vague measures. Programs do not acquire these qualities by accident; it is unreasonable to expect that we will intuitively create good software just because we are clever, experienced or able to write proper, structured code with lots of comments. It is my experience that there are three coding practices which can defeat the objective of good software. These are:

- functions that are too big
- functions that have many purposes
- functions that are tightly bound to the rest of the system

An oversized function might be defined as one that exceeds two pages of source code listing. This is not to say that all functions are going to be smaller than that, or that they should be. As with all rules, exceptions can be found. It is generally true, however, that big programs are more difficult to comprehend than small ones. Software is easier to understand if it is broken into small components. There are occasions when a function will necessarily be larger than you would like it to be. You will find examples of such functions in Appendix A.

Systems software, particularly on-line retrieval tools, must operate efficiently; this is the fourth measure of a good program. You can often improve the performance of a process by coding the discrete functions into an in-line code sequence. Each functional sequence of code is written and concatenated with ones before it. This process can eliminate the function calling overhead known as "context switching." Purists will be offended by this practice because it violates the small function discipline. So, when this is done, the individual code sequences should be identified with eye-catching comments to provide clarity of purpose.

Functions with many purposes are said to lack functional strength. A strong function has a single purpose, and its purpose is clear and explicit. Here is a simple example. A function that returns the square root of an argument is strong if that is all it does. You can muddy up the definition of the function's purpose by having it do something else as well, such as deposit the square root into a file record. The more of this you do, the weaker the code becomes.

A function that is tightly bound to the rest of the system weakens the entire system. If there are a lot of these, maintenance becomes a nightmare. A simple change in one part of the system can cause an undesired, unexpected and often undetected domino effect. The binding of functions can be loosened by the practice of information hiding.

Information Hiding

A software function can be described as having three basic components. These are:

- The input data
- The processing algorithm
- The result

In our software we are going to view each function in the light of not only what it is but also what it is not. If a single function in a major system has as its purpose the processing of some input data into a result, then there must also be a huge body of other information in the system with which the function is unconcerned. That information is to be hidden.

Consider a function that decides if a particular date falls in a leap year. In C, that function might look like this:

```
int leap (yr)
int yr;
{
  return !(yr % 400) || (!(yr % 4) && (yr % 100));
}
```

The function has a single input, the year of the date in question. Its process consists of an expression that returns a true (nonzero) value if the year is a leap year or false (zero) if the year is not a leap year. There is a single result, the true or false condition which results from the expression.

This function does not need any data other than the year being tested. It does not know whether the month is represented by another integer (1–12) or by the names of the months. Further, it should not be given the opportunity to change anything in the system other than the answer it is returning. It doesn't know whether it is being used in a payroll system or as part of an orbiting space laboratory, and it doesn't care. The rest of the data in the system is hidden from this function.

This simple example introduces the principle of "information hiding." A function can neither read nor write data outside of its own concern. Further, the complex data structures that underpin a function are not necessarily critical to its operation. Therefore, the function does not need to know about them.

In the software of our tool collection, there are many instances of information hiding. In one example, the cache memory functions are used to efficiently support the file management and B-tree management functions. Neither of these two subsystems knows or cares how cache memory is managed. That information is hidden from them. If there is no benefit to be gained by using the cache memory functions (perhaps the operating system already has the feature built in), then the cache memory functions can be replaced with ones that call the standard library file functions, and the system will still process properly.

Use of the tools in the collection involves the development of applications where a significant amount of the processing is done by the toolset functions. The details of that processing are hidden from the applications programs. You need not be concerned about the techniques used in the tools except to satisfy your own curiosity about the technology. By hiding these details, the collection allows you to turn your attention away from the tedious and routine concerns of the interactive environment and toward more important matters—the requirements of the user and the application system you are going to develop.

Software Tools

Software tool building is the concept that inspired the development of the functions in this work. A productive programmer is one with a modern, effective collection of software tools from which to select. This concept did not originate with the software here. The concept already existed; the software came about as the result of a need for specific tools for a specific application, and the realization that the tools to be developed could be useful for later software system development.

Perhaps we should examine the contents of a typical software tool collection. There are several categories of tools. First is the group of programs used to help us write and test code. There is a text processor for typing in our source code. The compiler, assembler, librarian, and linker are used to get the code into an executable form. An on-line debugger is helpful, and we need several utility programs, among them a file dump program and a source language cross reference program.

A second category of tools is the collection of existing programs used in the software system once it becomes operational. These are often called "utility" programs, and among them are the general purpose file sort, the file copy program and the mass storage backup program.

All of those programs are in our tool collection, and we wouldn't consider throwing any of them away. So why not extend the concept of frugality to the software we develop? That is what C software development tools represent, and that is the concept that we want to encourage, promote, and proliferate through their wide distribution and use.

The third category of software tools is the subject of this book. These are functions that are developed by the individual programmer to be reused. They range in size and complexity from tiny and simple to huge and complex. A function in this book called "movmem" moves one block of memory to another. It is just a few lines of code, and its processing is simple. Another function, "insert_key," inserts a caller-supplied string value into a complex balanced hierarchical structure of data indices. That function is large, and its processing is very complex. Certainly, once you have the big function you would never want to rewrite it. But, the same idea should be supplied to the small one as well. Software systems are made up of a lot of small and large functions; the more of them we can take from a library of tools, the fewer we have to rewrite.

The first two categories of software tools tend to be specific to the local installation. If we move to another environment, we adjust to the new editor, assembler, and so on. The third category is more personal. A programmer will take the tools to each new assignment and continue to reuse them and continue to build the collection.

Building a software tool requires discipline during its development. If you determine that some new software function is likely to be needed another time, you should develop it as a reusable tool. Here are the cardinal rules of software tool construction.

1. Make the function as independent of the particular current application as possible. Do not tie it to the specific data

structures of your application system or to the characteristics of the operating system.

2. Write it to be portable. If you are using a nonportable language, write the function with the basic control structures of structured programming so that the translation to another language will be easier.

3. Physically separate the function's source code from the programs that call it. Put the function in a library of tools if a software librarian program is available. You want to make the code readily available the next time you need it. If it is buried inside the source file of some application program, then you will forget you have it, forget where it is, or consider it less trouble to rewrite it than to dig it out.

As you proceed through the next several chapters of the features and functions of this tool collection, give thought to how they can help you with the next system you develop. Take a look at the last application you developed. Would any of what we have built here been relevant to that effort? Can any of what you designed there be incorporated into your own tool collection?

Summary of
C Software
Development Tools

3

This chapter contains a summary of the toolset functions; details are found in later chapters addressed to each of the subsystems. This summary does not include all of the functions in Appendix A. Rather, it lists the ones that will be called from the code you develop for the application. Others are used from within the toolset and are not called from applications programs. This summary can be used as a quick reference to the functions, the parameters they expect, and what each of them returns.

Some functions are defined as returning type ADDR, which is the variable type of a file address and is equated to the `long` variable type by a `#define` in the file "toolset.h." Other functions are type VOID. This, too, has a `#define` in "toolset.h" and is equated to the `void` return type for current compilers and to the `int` type for other compilers that do not support the void type.

All of the functions are declared in header files that are associated with each major subsystem. Since a function must be declared if it returns something other than an integer, it is prudent to include the appropriate header files in applications programs using toolset functions. Following is a list of header files that declare functions:

```
terminal.h
cache.h
file.h
menu.h
screen.h
sort.h
btree.h
```

Here is a summary of all of the functions with a brief description of the purpose of each.

Sub-routines	`movmem(s, d, ln)`	Moves a block of memory.
	`setmem(s, ln, n)`	Sets a block of memory to a character value.
	`fatal(n)`	Terminates processing with an error message.
	`execute(p, a1, a2)`	Executes a program.

Terminal-Dependent Functions	`VOID init_crt()`	Initializes the terminal.
	`int get_byte()`	Gets a byte from the keyboard.
	`VOID put_byte(c)`	Puts a byte to the screen.
	`VOID cursor(x,y)`	Positions the cursor.
	`VOID clr_scrn()`	Clears the screen.
	`VOID high_intensity(n)`	Sets intensity on/off.
	`VOID underline(n)`	Sets underline on/off.

Cache Memory Management Functions	`VOID init_cache()`	Initializes the cache buffers.
	`char *get_node(fd, p)`	Gets a node from cache.
	`VOID put_node(fd, p, buff)`	Puts a node to cache.
	`VOID release_node(fd, p, chgd)`	Releases a node to cache.
	`VOID flush_cache(fd)`	Flushes the cache buffers.

Data File Management Functions	`int opn_file(name, len)`	Opens a data file.
	`VOID cls_file(fd)`	Closes a data file.
	`ADDR new_record(fd, buff)`	Adds a record to a file.
	`int delete_record(fd, rcd_no)`	Deletes a record from a file.
	`int get_record(fd, rcd_no, buff)`	Gets a record from a file.
	`int put_record(fd, rcd_no, buff)`	Puts a record to a file.

Menu Management Functions	`VOID menu_exec(mp, keytab, banner)`	Executes the menu.
Screen Management Functions	`VOID read_screens(screen_name)`	Reads a file of screen definitions.
	`char scrn_proc(scrn_no, data, sw)`	Collects a screen of input data.
	`VOID err_msg(msg)`	Displays an error message.
	`VOID notice(msg)`	Displays a notice.
	`VOID clrmsg()`	Clears the message/notice line.
	`VOID backfill(crt, item, screen_data)`	Writes an item to the screen.
	`char get_item(scrn, crt, fld)`	Reads an item from the screen.
	`VOID reset_screens()`	Resets screen management system.
Sort Functions	`int init_sort(prms)`	Initializes the sort.
	`VOID sort(s_rcd)`	Passes records to sort.
	`char *sort_op()`	Retrieves sorted records.
	`VOID sort_stats()`	Displays sort statistics.
B-Tree Management Functions	`int init_b(tree, name, len)`	Initializes a B-tree index for use.
	`int close_b(tree)`	Closes a B-tree index file.
	`int find_key(tree, key, addr)`	Searches a B-tree for a key value.
	`int insert_key(tree,key,ad,sw)`	Inserts a key into a B-tree.
	`int delete_key(tree, key, addr)`	Deletes a key from a B-tree.
	`ADDR get_next(tree)`	Gets address of the next key.
	`ADDR get_prev(tree)`	Gets address of the previous key.
	`ADDR find_first(tree)`	Gets address of first key.
	`ADDR find_last(tree)`	Gets address of last key.

4 The Subroutines

This chapter is the first of several containing descriptions of the software in the tool collection. As I said in Chapter 2, we are starting at the bottom. A file in Appendix A called "subs.c" contains a set of subroutines used by most of the other functions. This is a description of those subroutines.

```
movmem (s, d, ln)
char *s, *d;
int ln;
```

Movmem is used to move a block of memory from one location to another. The character pointers s and d point to the source and destination memory locations, respectively. The integer ln is the number of bytes to move. Be careful about this function. Some C compilers include a similar function. The Aztec compiler has a function with the same name and parameter sequence, but it does not work in this system. This function checks to see if overlapping memory addresses are specified and selects either a forward or backward move sequence depending upon the relationship of the two starting addresses. The BDS C compiler has a movmem function that works this way, and when these functions were ported to the Aztec compiler, movmem was rewritten.

Movmem is used extensively by the B-tree subsystem to shift strings of keys and file pointers around when keys are inserted and deleted and when nodes are split and combined. The performance of the B-tree functions could be improved if movmem were rewritten in assembly language.

41

```
setmem (s, ln, n)
char *s, n;
int ln;
```

This is a function to set an area of memory (pointed to by **s**) with a length of **ln** to a value consisting of all bytes equal to **n**. Some C compilers include this function, or have one with a similar name, but it is included here in case yours doesn't.

```
fatal (n)
int n;
```

This is the standard fatal error message function. It is called when an error has occurred that the software can't handle. There are only nine such errors, and they usually mean that code must be modified to correct the error. These are not error messages that the user should expect to see. When they do appear, you will get a call, and you will have to fix something.

The fatal function prints the error number and the message and terminates execution of the program. Some of these descriptions assume that you have already read the chapters on the various subsystems. Use this section as a reference when you debug your code. The errors are:

Error ts001: Insufficient memory for cache

There is not enough memory left for the Cache functions to allocate buffers. Try reducing the number of cache nodes (MXNODES in cache.c) or otherwise reducing the size of the program.

Error ts002: Disk i/o error

An unrecoverable disk error is encountered by the cache management functions. This problem concerns your hardware or media. This error is rarely seen, because the operating systems usually intervene with their own messages before returning to the calling function.

Error ts003: Index file not properly closed

When opening a B-tree index, it was found to have been left open from the last time it was used. Either the b__close function was not called or, perhaps, a power failure occurred. The index must be rebuilt, or, if it is certain that no changes were made to the index, the unlock program can be run against the index.

Error ts004: Cannot find template file

Read__screens was passed the name of a screen template file that doesn't exist.

Error ts005: Insufficient memory for screens

The function read__screens allocates blocks of memory for screen templates. The number of bytes to be allocated per template is specified by the global symbol SCBUFF in "screen.h." A screen template file can contain templates for more than one screen image, and a block of memory is allocated for each template in the file. If not enough memory exists, read__screens calls fatal with this error. Either the program must be shortened or more memory must be provided.

Error ts006: Cannot find program

This is called from the Menu Management functions when a specified program name doesn't exist. Take a look at what was specified in the menu structure. The execl function for Aztec CII under CP/M-80 automatically appends the .COM file type to the name. But, since there can be .COM files and .EXE files under MS-DOS, Aztec C86 requires that the caller supply the file type.

Error ts007: Screen buffer is too small

A screen definition has more characters in the ASCII template than allowed by the global symbol SCBUFF in the file "screen.h." The offending template can be shortened, or the size allowed by SCBUFF can be increased.

Error ts008: Insufficient memory for files

The system has run out of memory during file processing. You must either shorten the program or provide more memory to the process.

Error ts009: Insufficient memory for B-trees

The system has run out of memory during B-tree processing. Again, you must either shorten the program or provide more memory to the process.

```
int execute (p, a1, a2)
char *p, *a1, *a2;
```

This function executes a "child" process from the calling program. A child process is one that returns to the executing or "parent" process upon completion. The child returns a completion to the parent. Each of the compilers I have used implement the process differently. Since the various compilers use different function names and different conventions for the passing of parameters, this function provides a common and consistent interface for all of the subsystems. The function is compiled differently depending on which compiler is used as defined by the global symbol COMPILER in the source file "toolset.h".

The caller passes a pointer to the name of the program to be executed in the pointer variable **p**. This name must include a file extension of .com or .exe. The character pointers **a1** and **a2** point to the first two parameters on the command line for the child program. These correspond to the two command line parameters **argv[1]** and **argv[2]** which are passed to the main function of a C program when it is executed.

Summary

By implementing these functions, we have the bottom of the software development tool collection. So far, we cannot do anything meaningful because all we have are some utility functions. But, ground has been broken, and the toolset is underway. Chapter 5 deals with the next level up: the functions to implement the keyboard and video screen displays of our computer.

5 Terminal-Dependent Functions

This chapter deals with the characteristics of the computer's terminal device, the hardware consisting of the video screen, and the keyboard. Every terminal model is different, and software packages must be compatible with most of the popular models if the software is to be portable. A personal computer either connects to one of the commercially available terminals (such as the ADM/ 3A) with a standard serial input/output interface or, as in the IBM PC, has the screen and keyboard interfaces as an integral part of the computer system with a direct keyboard input port and a row and column array of video refresh memory, directly addressed by the processor.

Commercial portable software usually includes an installation procedure that, among other things, allows the terminal device to be specified. The installation procedure installs tables or software device drivers to address the terminal. Depending upon the complexity of the software package, the differences between terminal drivers can be significant. Some packages ignore the problem and treat all terminals the same. Screens are cleared by scrolling everything off the top, cursors are never positioned, and so on. We cannot take so simple an approach. The screen management and menu management functions need to drive the video display efficiently, and they use function keys. To do that requires the use of the features of the screen and the keyboard.

There are seven terminal functions that must be coded for the specific terminal device to be used. These are:

- initialize the terminal
- read a character
- write a character
- position the cursor
- clear the screen
- set the intensity to high or low
- set the underline mode on or off

This code can be developed without regard to portability because the functions are hardware-dependent and they are small. Functionality should be more important than portability. In this book, the terminal software uses the protocols implemented by the ANSI.SYS driver included with MS-DOS. These aren't the most efficient terminal drivers; the displays would be faster if terminal.c were written in assembly language. That has not been done here because the various C compilers for the IBM PC use assemblers with different source language formats.

Why are terminal character input and output functions needed when C already has getchar and putchar in the standard library? The standard input/output functions don't always do what this software requires. Some terminals have multiple character protocols for special operations such as intensity changes and function key values. The toolset software uses single key values for the function keys and single function calls to change intensity. By localizing the terminal operations in functions that are called from the toolset functions, we can support any protocol and still retain portability in the rest of the software.

The terminal-dependent source code in this book assumes that the ANSI.SYS device handler is installed. If you are using that configuration, refer to the MS-DOS manual for an explanation of how to install the ANSI.SYS handler. The ANSI protocols use multiple character sequences for screen and cursor control actions. The function keys and cursor keys from the IBM PC keyboard are also used.

The functions that read and write the keyboard and screen call the standard C library function names `getchar` and `putchar`. In many C compilers, these functions do more than provide simple, unadorned console input/output. Adorned input/output is not wanted here; rather, the functions should get and put characters from and to the console, and input characters should not be echoed to the screen. Input characters should also be returned to the calling function as soon as the key is pressed. Some of the compiler library functions collect input characters in a buffer until the Return key is pressed. So, the calls to `getchar` and `putchar` must be replaced with calls that do simple, unadorned terminal input and ouput. Some compilers have direct DOS function calls, and these can be used to directly address the keyboard and screen. So that they might be used, a `#define` macro substitution replaces `getchar` and `putchar` with the appropriate DOS call. This is how it is done for the Aztec C86 compiler on the IBM PC with MS-DOS:

```
#define getchar() bdos(7,0,0)
#define putchar(c) bdos(2,c,0)
```

For other compilers or other operating systems, similar steps might be necessary. The software in this book can be compiled with the DeSmet C compiler, Aztec C86, and the Lattice C compiler, and there are `#if` preprocessor statements in workshop.h to make the proper substitutions for `getchar` and `putchar` based upon the compiler.

Remember that these techniques are nonportable; we use them only for software in hardware-dependent modules, and any such dependencies are hidden in functions that have independent calling conventions. The large majority of these functions and all applications functions are unaffected by the hardware dependencies and do not need to be modified when the terminal drivers are changed.

Terminal Example

Here is a simple program to illustrate the use of the terminal functions. It can be used to test a new version of terminal.c that has been rewritten for a different terminal configuration. The example program "termexmp.c" (Listing 5-1) initializes the terminal, clears the screen, positions the cursor in the approximate center of a 24-row by 80-column screen, and asks the user to type a function key. Using the global definitions from the file "keys.h" (in Appendix A), the program displays the name of the function key that is pressed with full intensity and underlining. It continues to do this until ESCAPE is pressed. If this program works, "terminal.c" is correct.

```
/* ------------------- termexmp.c -------------------- */

#include (stdio.h)
#include "toolset.h"
#include "terminal.h"
#include "keys.h"

main()
{
    char c = 0;
    int k;
    static int kyv [] = {F1,F2,F3,F4,F5,F6,F7,F8,F9,F10,
                UP,FWD,INSERT,DELETE,0};
    static char *kys [] = {"F1","F2","F3","F4","F5","F6","F7","F8",
                "F9","F10","UP","FWD","INSERT","DELETE",
                "not a function key"};

    init_crt();                             /* initialize the terminal  */
    clr_scrn();                             /* clear the screen         */
    while (c != ESC)    {
        cursor(20,10);                      /* position the cursor      */
        dsp("Press a function key...");     /* (never tell the user     */
                                            /*      to hit the computer) */
        put_byte(c = get_byte());           /* read a character and echo */
        if (c == ESC)
            continue;
        k = 0;
        while (c != kyv [k] && kyv [k] != 0)
            k++;
        cursor(20,11);
        dsp("Your entry was            ");
        high_intensity(TRUE);                 /* bright              */
        underline(TRUE);                      /* underlined          */
        cursor(35,11);
        dsp(kys [k]);                         /* display what was pressed */
        high_intensity(FALSE);                /* dim                 */
        underline(FALSE);                     /* plain               */
    }
}

/* ------ write a string to the terminal -------------- */

dsp(s)
char *s;
{
    while(*s)
        put_byte(*s++);
}
```

Listing 5-1.

Terminal Functions

These functions control the screen and keyboard. To use them, include the following statements in a calling program:

```
#include <toolset.h>
#include <terminal.h>
#include <keys.h>
```

```
VOID init_crt ()
```

This function initializes the terminal. It includes a flag to tell it if it has ever been called. If so, it does nothing. Some terminals require an initializing sequence, and this is the place to do it. It calls the clear screen (clr__scrn) function before it returns.

```
char get_byte ()
```

This function reads a keystroke. It returns the keyed value to the caller. If the terminal sends multiple character sequences for special keystrokes, a translated single unique value is to be returned. The values for all special keystrokes (for example, cursor arrow keys) are found in "keys.h."

```
VOID put_byte (c)
char c;
```

This function writes a character to the terminal. If the terminal requires multiple character sequences for special functions, such as cursor up, backspace, and tab, put translate logic into this function, because the toolset functions send single character values for these operations as defined in keys.h.

```
VOID cursor (x,y)
int x, y;
```

This function places the cursor at the coordinates specified by x and y: x is the cursor column and y is the row. The upper left (northwest) corner of the screen is cursor location 0,0.

VOID clr_scrn ()

This function clears the screen. When using the screen management functions, always use this function for clearing the screen. The function includes an external variable that the screen manager uses to indicate which screen template is currently displayed. That way, the template is not unnecessarily redisplayed. If the screen is cleared and the variable is not, the screen manager might think that a particular template is still on the screen.

VOID high_intensity (n)

If n is TRUE, then all subsequent characters written to the terminal are at full intensity. If n is FALSE, half intensity is used. If the terminal does not support dual intensity, this function should be null.

VOID underline (n)

If n is TRUE, the terminal is put into underline mode. If n is FALSE, the underline mode is turned off. Some terminals do not have character underlining. The software in this book assumes use of the IBM PC monochrome monitor (or an equivalent). The color graphics board of the PC does not support underlined characters. The preprocessor conditional global COLOR (in "terminal.c") must be equated to TRUE to indicate use of this board. It causes the underline character to be displayed whenever a blank is written to the screen while underline mode is turned on. This way, an underlined field looks like this:

    __underlined_data__

Summary

With the completion of the subroutines and the terminal functions, the toolset foundation is under way, and we can proceed up to the next level in our "bottom–up" journey. The next group of functions to be discussed is developed around a concept adapted from hardware architecture. It is a software implementation of "cache memory." Chapter 6 presents a full discussion and implementation of this concept.

Cache
Memory

One more level is required to complete the foundation of the software development toolset. To support fast access of disk files of data and indices, a way is needed to improve the performance of the retrieval of random data. To achieve that improvement, I have taken a hardware architecture, called "cache memory," from the bigger systems and emulated it in software.

The cache memory subsystem is used by the B-tree functions and the file record management functions. It is not likely that it will be needed for other than these two purposes; however, there might be occasions where the processing overhead of the file record management functions (Chapter 7) would be excessive, and it might be appropriate for an application to call cache directly.

The cache memory subsystem is a collection of C functions that use random access memory (RAM) as a cache buffer for disk records. This is an efficiency maneuver used when there are frequent random accesses to files with fixed length records. It returns a substantial benefit when the use of the file causes some records to be accessed more often than others.

This caching technique is very much like the BUFFERS option provided by MS-DOS. For users of that operating system, the advantages of the cache memory subsystem are minimal. In other environments, (CP/M, for example) there are significant performance improvements when the caching algorithms are applied. MS-DOS users will realize some improvement when there is enough memory to allow the caching of more than the 255 disk records imposed as a maximum by the BUFFERS option. This, of course, would be relevant in large, complex systems of multiple data and index files with large numbers of records.

The caching algorithms use RAM to buffer disk records. When records are requested by the application software, they are read into RAM and passed to the caller. When they are no longer needed by the caller, they are saved in a queue of released data. Subsequent requests for a particular record cause that record to be retrieved from RAM rather than from disk. New records added by the application go into the queue also. When the queue is full and a record buffer is required, the cache software uses a "least recently used" algorithm to appropriate the space containing the oldest record in the queue. This technique is based upon the theory that frequently used records will continue to be used frequently and infrequently used records will continue to be used infrequently. Of course, when a space is appropriated, its record contents must be preserved. The old record that it contains is written back to disk if it has been changed since originally read into the cache buffer. It is also written back if it is in the cache as an addition to the file.

The B-tree functions (Chapter 11) were written by using cache memory. A B-tree has a header record, a root record, and lower levels of "nodes" and "leaves." The root and header records tend to be read and written more frequently than the nodes and leaves. The higher the node is in the hierarchy, the more often it is accessed. This pattern of frequent and infrequent access is exactly the environment where caching enhances the performance of retrievals.

The B-tree subsystem could have been developed with the file record management functions to do the input and output of nodes and leaves. But, since the purpose of B-trees is to achieve processing efficiency, it is better to avoid the file record manager overhead and deal directly with the cache. If you find yourself facing a similar decision, you will need to know how cache memory works.

The Cache Theory

Cached records are not to be confused with the file records discussed in the next chapter. Where file records have different lengths in different files, cached records are always the same length and are usually related to physical disk sectors. We call these cached records "nodes."

Cache memory is established initially with a set of nodes that, upon execution of a using program, are empty. The size of a node is determined by the global definition NODELEN in the file "toolset.h." This is the same definition for the length of a B-tree node. The two length definitions are inseparable because B-tree functions use direct cache calls to manage nodes. A node is 512 bytes long, and cache can manage 25 of them. The value 25 is defined by MXNODES in the source file "cache.c." The values for NODELEN and MXNODES can be changed. The more nodes that can be saved in RAM, the fewer disk accesses must be endured during random file accesses. MS-DOS users can defer the caching operation to the MS-DOS BUFFERS option by making MXNODES a small number such as 5.

Each node represents a pseudophysical disk sector from a data file. We say "pseudo" because C does not recognize sectors as such, and the low-level file functions in the standard library are independent of hardware or operating system sector sizes. For the sake of the B-tree functions, NODELEN should be an even multiple of the disk sector. This choice will probably make it run faster depending on the operating system and its implementation of physical disk input and output. The IBM PC and its compatibles have a sector length of 512 bytes.

What is done with a node? Mainly, it is read from disk, saved in RAM, and written to disk. A node is numbered starting with one and is related to the file descriptor (fd) of the file it is in. The fd is the integer value returned by the file open function. (This value specifically refers to the integer returned by the open functions of the C standard library, not of the file management functions. Remember that cache memory is at a lower level, between the file management functions above and the standard library functions below.) When a caller first requests a specific node, cache reads it into one of its buffers and passes the caller a pointer to it.

The node buffer consists of an array of nodes, and each node resides in one of three lists: a "free nodes" list, an "in-use" list, and a "released" list. The lists take the form of the "linked list" data structure. A linked list is a structure where entries in a table (or records in a file) are serially connected by data pointers. Each entry has pointers to two other entries, the one ahead of it in the list and the one following it. The list starts with a "list head" containing pointers to the first and last entries in the list. The first entry points to the next, which points to the next, and so on; whereas, the last entry points to the one before it, which points to the one before that, and so on. The sequence of a list is unrelated to the coincidental proximity of each entry to the others. A given table can have several linked lists, each one threading a different path through the table. The last entry in a list has a NULL forward list pointer value to indicate the end of the list, while the first entry has a NULL reverse list pointer value to indicate the beginning entry in the list.

Figure 6-1 illustrates the cache memory pool of nodes and its three linked lists. The nodes consist of the list pointers and pointers to buffers that have been allocated for the disk data asigned to the nodes. Each node also contains the file and sector numbers related to the data in the node and a flag that indicates if there have been changes in the data since originally read from the disk. The list pointers are shown as integer offsets for clarity of the illustration. Actually, they and the memory pointers are character pointers in the idiom of the C language.

The first linked list in the cache memory node pool is the list of unused or free buffers. Initially all nodes are in this list. The second list lists buffers that contain nodes that are in use by the caller. The third list gives nodes that have been released by the caller to cache memory.

The unused list gets shorter as nodes are moved into the in-use list. Then, as they are released, they are moved into the released list. Nodes are returned to the unused list when the cache memory node pool is flushed, usually at the end of a process or at regular intervals. Flushing is the process where all in-memory cached data is returned to disk storage. Its execution is caused by a function call from the application.

The movement of nodes between lists does not involve the actual movement of the nodes themselves or the data in the node buffers. Instead, the list pointers are changed to logically assign a node to the appropriate list without actually moving the data in the node.

As long as there are unused nodes, a caller's request for a node is filled from that list. Callers ask for nodes by requesting the data in a particular disk sector or by passing a buffer of data to be writ-

LIST HEADS:

	FIRST	LAST
FREE	6	10
IN-USE	4	2
RELEASED	1	3

NODE POOL:

NODE #	PREV	File/Sect/Chgd/Buff	NEXT
1	NULL		3
2	5		NULL
3	1		NULL
4	NULL		5
5	4		2
6	NULL		7
7	6		8
8	7		9
9	8		10
10	9		NULL

Figure 6-1. The cache memory pool of nodes and its three linked lists.

ten to the disk into a specified sector. When no nodes are in the unused list, requests are filled from the released list.

Data in the released list either originally came from disk or was given to cache memory to be written to disk as a new sector. The actual disk write occurs only when the space occupied by the data is required to service a request for another node and then only if the released data in the node was a new sector or was marked as having been changed by the caller.

When cache services a request for a node, it first looks to see if the record from the specified sector is already in a node in the released list. If so, this node is transferred to the in-use list and a pointer to it is passed to the caller. If the record from the sector is not in a node in the released list, node space is appropriated, the disk record for the requested sector is read into the node, and a pointer to the node is passed to the caller.

The appropriation of a node, when done, uses a least recently used algorithm. This means that cache always appropriates the node that has been on the released list longer than any other. This way, sectors that have a high frequency of activity stay near the top of the list and remain in memory. The header and root nodes of a B-tree exhibit this property and will not be read from and written to disk as often as other nodes.

A caller may add a new sector to the file. This call gets a node buffer and copies the caller's data into it. The buffer is put into the released list and is marked as having been changed.

The cache functions are not particularly defensive against incorrect calls. Illogical requests of the cache functions can deliver odd results. An application should not make multiple retrievals of the same sector without intervening releases of it. In other words, an application may only have one copy of a given sector at a time. Further, the number of concurrent in-use nodes must be kept at or below the maximum capacity as specified by the global definition MAXNODES in "toolset.h." A sector that does not exist should not be requested, and cache memory should not be requested for a file that has not been opened. Do not release a node you don't have. A calling program is expected to release all nodes it has requested, and, finally, it should be sure to flush the cache buffers when it is finished processing. Note that cached records are held in memory until they are flushed or until the space occupied by one of them is appropriated. Thus unflushed sectors are lost if the system goes down. This is a problem that is common to all record buffering schemes.

If this all seems unduly harsh, remember that cache memory is a systems programming tool. Its primary function is to support the file and B-tree managers, and these subsystems do not violate these rules. It must, by definition, be as efficient as possible. It does not use the error-trapping measures required by other tools because it should be applied in a very terse and concise environment. The overhead of bulletproof code would compromise the requirements for efficiency of memory space and processing time.

Cache Memory Functions

These functions are used by the caller to manage buffers by using the cache memory functions. There is no example program for the cache memory functions because an excellent understanding of their use can be gained by a careful reading of the code associated with the B-tree functions. To use these functions, include the following statements in the calling program's source file:

```
#include <toolset.h>
#include <cache.h>
```

```
init_cache ()
```

This function is called prior to any of the other cache memory functions. Its purpose is to initialize the cache memory node structures. There must be a call to this function so that memory is allocated for the nodes. The toolset functions that use cache take care of this: but, it doesn't matter if unnecessary calls to init__cache are made. If cache memory has already been initialized, then init__cache simply returns.

```
char *get_node (fd, p)
int fd;
ADDR p;
```

Use this function to get a node from cache. Remember a node is a block of data with a length defined by the global NODELEN in the file "toolset.h." The parameter **p** identifies the requested node. It is a variable of type ADDR (also defined in "toolset.h") that numbers the nodes relative to one. The **fd** parameter is the **fd** of the file being accessed. It is the value that is returned when the file is opened and that cache must use to access the file functions of the standard C library. The function returns a character pointer that points to the node's data sector. Cache maintains all node buffers in a memory pool and allows callers to work in that space. If you call any of these functions with a constant **p**, remember to use a cast operator to force the constant into type ADDR. For example:

```
ptr = get_node (fd, (ADDR) 5);
```

```
put_node (fd, p, buff)
int fd;
ADDR p;
char *buff;
```

Use this function to add a new node to the file. The parameters fd and p are the same as in get_node. The buff parameter is a pointer to the caller's memory location containing the new file node. If the sector already exists on the file, its contents are replaced by the data pointed to by buff.

```
release_node (fd, p, chgd)
int fd;
ADDR p;
int chgd;
```

This function is called when the caller is done with a node that was retrieved by using get_node. The parameter chgd is a flag with the values of TRUE or FALSE (1 or 0). If the flag is TRUE, then the caller has changed some data in the node and wants it rewritten to disk before its space is reused or when the cache buffers are flushed (see next discussion on flush_cache). If the flag is FALSE then the data values have not changed, and it is not necessary that the node be updated.

```
flush_cache (fd)
int fd;
```

This function flushes cache buffers by forcing them to be written to disk. If fd is NULL, then all cache buffers are flushed; otherwise, only those buffers associated with the specified file fd are flushed. Use this function at the end of any program that has changed data by using cache nodes.

Summary

The foundation of our software tool collection is complete. We have some subroutines, the terminal drivers, and a cache memory. In Chapter 7 I present the first in a series of several subsystems that you can call directly from your interactive application software. This first subsystem contains the file management functions.

7

Data
File
Management

All of the lower-level functions are now in place. In this chapter I introduce the first set of functions that you call from your applications code. These are the data file management functions—the ones that manage the kind of random-access files that are an integral part of the interactive environment. Let's begin by looking at what we get from the C standard library and what the deficiencies are in those functions. Then, we can consider what the toolset has to offer as an improvement.

In the C standard input/output library functions, a file record is addressed by the location of the first byte of the record relative to the first byte of the file. So, if the records are, say, 75 bytes long, and the third record is required, it is addressed by character position 150. Record number one is at location 0, number two is 75 bytes away at location 75 and number three is at location 150. This is the UNIX view of data files, and it is understandable that it would proliferate wherever the C standard library is used. In almost all other environments, a file of data is viewed as a collection of logical records rather than of characters.

A "logical" record address identifies where the record resides relative to the other records in the file. In the example of the 75 byte record, the logical address of the third record is 3; its character location is 150. It seems natural to want to address it by its logical record number, not by its byte location in the file. So, if you want record number 30, you can call for it by record number 30. This makes for more understandable software and more comprehensible data structures. Software and computers are complex enough. If we hide these system-dependent details inside of our toolset functions, we allow ourselves to think and work at a higher, more problem-oriented level of abstraction. Our productivity is enhanced because our tools and techniques are effective.

A data record is a collection of data elements organized into a fixed format (assuming a fixed length record, of course). A file is a collection of records. The length of the record is the sum of the lengths of its data elements plus any padding that might occur because of the automatic alignment of certain multiple-byte data types. The address of a record is usually considered to be an integer relative to the position the record holds in the file. The first record is number 1, the second record is number 2, and so on. So, the character location of a record in a file is computed as the (record number minus one) times the length. This number gives a character position relative to zero which is what the standard C functions named **seek** and **fseek** expect. Therefore, if what you start with is the record number, you must compute the record position to use the C library functions.

It is more natural to address a record in a random-access file by its logical record number. Hashing algorithms, which involve computing a random number from the data components of the key data element, usually deliver a logical record number rather than a byte position. Other access techniques, such as inverted indices, can manage a larger file size more efficiently if they can deal with a record number rather than a character position. For example, if there are 50,000 records of 100 bytes each, the record number can be contained in a 16-bit unsigned integer; but, the character position, which can reach from 0 to 4,999,999, requires a long integer (32 bits on MS-DOS systems).

The deletion of a record from a random file presents another set of considerations. Perhaps the system allows a file to grow as records are added without trying to reuse the space of previously deleted records. If so, the file just keeps getting larger and larger as records are added. With such an approach, the number of records required for a personnel file is equal to the number of employees the company has ever had including everyone who has quit, died, retired, or been fired (or become a consultant). This fact is because the system isn't reusing the record space. If the file has little activity, it will be a while before the wasted space becomes a problem. But, eventually, disk space will run out. To avoid this, a system must reuse deleted record space. The file service functions in the C standard library do not provide for the reuse of disk space, so the toolset provides the capability.

Several ways are used to account for reusable record space in a random-access file. One way is to maintain a bit map with one bit for each possible record in the file. The state (1 or 0) of the bit tells the system if the record space is available or in use. To use that approach, you must know in advance how many records you might have, or else you must build a bit map structure that grows with the file. A second approach is to build a linked list of deleted records: that method is chosen for the toolset.

You learned in Chapter 6 that a linked list is a data structure consisting of data pointers. The first pointer is in a fixed location so that it can always be found. This pointer is called the "list head." It points to the first record which points to the next, and so on, until, at the end of the list, the last pointer points nowhere. Figure 7-1 is an example of the linked list used to keep track of reusable deleted record space. It shows a data file with 10 data records numbered 1 through 10. Records 2, 3, 6, 7, and 9 have been deleted. If you follow the list, you can reconstruct the sequence in which they were deleted. Starting with the first pointer in the list head, we proceed to record 7 which, using its next pointer, takes us to record 2. The trek through the deleted records follows the path 7, 2, 9, 6, 3. Record 3 ends the list, because it has a NULL (0) in its next pointer. We learned that the linked list nodes for cache memory use pointers to the previous entry as well as the next in the list. Here, however, the deleted record linked list only needs the pointer to the next record; entries are merely added to and removed from the beginning of the list. The end of the list is unimportant to the gathering of reusable record space. It doesn't care about the age of the space the way the least-recently-used algorithm of cache memory does.

The list head for the reusable record space linked list is placed at the beginning of the file in a header record. The **next** record pointers are put into the deleted records themselves, so no extra disk space is used for the list. The list head points to the first record in the list, and each record points to the next record in the list. Then, the last record in the list has NULL (0) to indicate the end of the list. The deleted records are marked with a −1 delete flag following the linked list record pointer. This flag can be used by a program that needs to read the file serially, thus bypassing

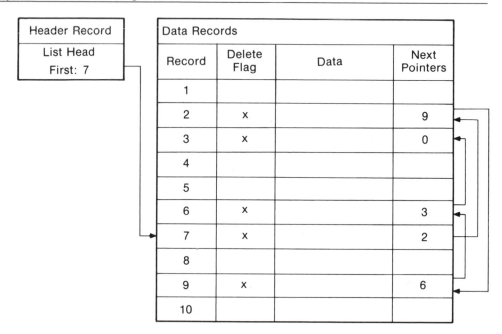

Header Record	Data Records			
List Head First: 7	Record	Delete Flag	Data	Next Pointers
	1			
	2	x		9
	3	x		0
	4			
	5			
	6	x		3
	7	x		2
	8			
	9	x		6
	10			

**Figure 7-1. Linked list to keep track of
reusable deleted record space.**

deleted records. It is also useful as a diagnostic aid during debugging.

When a record is deleted, the file management software remembers its location in the linked list of reusable records. When a record is to be added, the software looks to see if any deleted record space is available. If so, it is used for the new record. If not, the record is added to the end of the file.

The functions in this chapter take care of the issues we have discussed. All we need to know is the file name and, at the time the file is created, its record length. Then we can read, write, and delete records for which we know the record number, and we can add new records and let the function tell us what the new record number is.

We have acquired a significant addition to our tool kit with these functions. They give us freedom from care about low-level file space management. By hiding such details in the toolset, we can concentrate our development time on the concerns of the application we are building.

Data File Management Example

Listing 7-1 is a small data entry program that uses the functions of data file management. It creates and maintains a file of names. You can add, change, and delete records in the file. When you add a record, the program tells you what record number it assigned. When you change or delete a record, you must tell the program the record number to change or delete. The program tells you the name it found in the record you selected. Then, if you are changing, you must enter a new name. If you are deleting, the program deletes the record. There is not a lot of utility in such a small program other than to show you how to use the functions, so that is its purpose. To run the program type its name, fileexmp.

```c
/* --------------------- fileexmp.c --------------------------- */

#include <stdio.h>
#include "toolset.h"
#include "file.h"
#include "terminal.h"
long atol();
ADDR adr;
char name [25];
int fd;

main()
{
    char c = 0;
    if ((fd = opn_file("names.dat", 0)) == ERROR)
        fd = opn_file("names.dat", sizeof(name));
    while (c != '4')    {
        printf("\n\n 1 = add\n 2 = change\n 3 = delete\n 4 = quit\n)");
        put_byte(c = get_byte());
        switch (c) {
            case '1':    gtnam();
                         adr = new_record(fd, name);
                         printf("\nRecord # = %d", (int) adr);
                         break;
            case '2':    if (gtrno())    {
                             gtnam();
                             put_record(fd, adr, name);
                         }
                         break;
            case '3':    if (gtrno())
                             delete_record(fd, adr);
            default:     break;
        }
    }
    cls_file(fd);
}
```

Listing 7-1.

Listing 7-1 (continued)

```
gtnam()
{
    printf("\nEnter name: ");
    gets(name);
}

int gtrno()
{
    char r [5];
    int an, *d = (int *) name;
    printf("\nEnter Record #: ");
    gets(r);
    adr = (ADDR) atol(r);
    if (an = (get_record(fd, adr, name) == OK && *d != -1))
        printf("\nName in record %d = %s", (int) adr, name);
    else
        printf("\n??");
    return an;
}
```

Data File Management Functions

These are the functions used by the caller to manage files under the data file management subsystem. To use these, you must also implement the cache functions described in the previous chapter. Your calling program's source file should have the following statements:

```
#include <toolset.h>
#include <file.h>
```

```
int opn_file (name, len)
char *name;
int len;
```

This function is called to open an existing random file or to create a new one. If the caller expects a file to already exist, the value for the len parameter must be zero. In this case, if no file exists with the specified name, the function returns ERROR. Otherwise it opens the file and returns an integer that identifies the file and tells the other data file management functions which file to process. The returned value must be stored by the caller in a safe place to be available for later use. It is the toolset equivalent of the C library FILE pointer or the MS-DOS file "handle." If, when opn_file is called, the len parameter contains a nonzero value, then the function creates a new file with a record length as specified by len. Otherwise, when an existing file is opened, the software in these functions expects it to have been created by a call to this function.

Note, not just any file of fixed length records can be managed by these functions. There is a header record at the beginning of each file with an offset that locates the next available logical record number. The offset is built by this function. The header also defines the length of the record and contains a listhead that points to the linked list of deleted records. So, files to be maintained by these functions must have been originally built by this function. Here is what the file header looks like:

```
struct fil_hdr  {
        ADDR fst_rcd;  /* first available deleted record */
        ADDR nxt_rcd;  /* next available record position */
        int rcd_len;   /* length of record */
};
```

The data in the file immediately follows this record. The data consists of fixed-length records of the size specified by the integer rcd_len in the file header. The variable named fst_rcd is the linked list head pointer to the first record in the deleted record list. The variable nxt_rcd is the logical record number of the highest record number in the file plus one. It is used to add records to the file and to determine the end of file during a serial pass of the data records.

The system has a maximum number of files that can be opened by a calling program. This maximum is defined by the global symbol MAXFILES, which is found in the source file "files.c." When a caller attempts to open more files than this maximum, the function returns ERROR. The source code compiles a structure with two integers and one ADDR for each file allowed. On the IBM PC, where ADDR is a long integer, this comes to 8 bytes per file: so, there isn't much penalty in increasing the value of MAX-FILES.

You should be aware that some compilers limit the number of files that can be open at one time. This limit becomes a problem in a data base environment where you will want to have several data files and several B-tree index files open. Most compilers that run under MS-DOS allow this limit to be modified by a FILES = entry in a boot configuration file called CONFIG.SYS.

```
cls_file (fd)
int fd;
```

This function closes a file. It is necessary that it be called if any changes have been made to the data in the file either through record addition or modification. Call the function when all processing of the file is completed by the calling program. The parameter `fd` is the integer that was returned by the function `opn_file`.

```
ADDR new_record (fd, buff)
int fd;
char *buff;
```

This function creates a new record in the file. The parameter `fd` is the integer returned by `opn_file`. Buff is the address of the buffer of data. It is the caller's responsibility to assure that the size of buff is appropriate to the record size for the file. This function does not terminate the transfer of data on the null string terminator. Rather, it transfers as many bytes as the file expects in a record regardless of the data values of the bytes.

The function returns the logical record address assigned to the new record. A calling program might use this in the building of indices into the record. The logical record address is relative to one.

```
int delete_record (fd, rcd_no)
int fd;
ADDR rcd_no;
```

This function deletes the specified record from the file. The parameter `fd` identifies the file as it does in the other functions. Rcd_no is the logical record number to be deleted. This corresponds to the value returned by the function **new_record**. The logical record number is put into the deleted record linked list for the file, and the record is cleared and marked with a linked list record pointer and a delete flag containing the value −1. It is the caller's responsibility to assure that subsequent retrievals use the delete flag to know that a record has been deleted. Remember, this is a random access file and these are relatively low-level functions. The assumption is that a higher-level process is policing the integrity of the inverted indices into the file.

If the specified record number has never been assigned, the function returns ERROR. Otherwise it returns OK.

```
int get_record (fd, rcd_no, buff)
int fd;
ADDR rcd_no;
char *buff;
```

This function is called to retrieve an existing record from the file. As usual, `fd` identifies the file and `rcd_no` identifies the record. `Buff` points to the buffer into which the data record is to be transferred. It is the responsibility of the calling program to assure that `buff` is big enough to receive the full record. The record length was specified when the file was originally created by `opn_file`. If the specified record number has never been assigned, the function returns ERROR. Otherwise it returns OK.

This function gets a record even if the logical record, as identified by `rcd_no`, has been deleted. The deleted record is marked by the value −1 at the beginning of the record. The −1 is in a variable of type ADDR as defined in a `#define` statement in "toolset.h." This is useful for calling programs that need to pass the file in serial fashion, perhaps as an extract process, a back-up procedure, or to copy the file to another file or device. A serial pass of the file can use calls to `get_record` beginning with `rcd_no = 1` and incrementing `rcd_no` until the function returns ERROR. Records with the −1 would be ignored. This technique for reading a file in its physical sequence is less efficient than using the `read` function from the standard C library. The data file management functions are primarily used to access records in a random sequence. They work best when used this way. A program that needs to access records serially can use the `read` function if it first bypasses the data file management record header at the beginning of the file. The header is described as the structure `filhdr` in the source file "filhdr.h." A later chapter on file sorting includes a program that does what was just described.

```
int put_record (fd, rcd_no, buff)
int fd;
ADDR rcd_no;
char *buff;
```

This function is called to rewrite an existing record to the file. An existing record is defined as one that has been added to the file by the function new_record and has not yet been deleted by delete_record.

It is not necessary that you precede this function call by a call to get_record. If you do, it is not required that the record buffer be the same as that used for get_record or that any of the data be the same. This function will simply write the data from buff into the file identified by fd at the logical record position specified by rcd_no. If the specified record number has never been assigned, the function returns ERROR. Otherwise it returns OK. However, this function does not object if you put a record to a deleted record number. The data will be written, but some later call to the new_record function will reuse the space assigned to this logical record number. Furthermore, if you do rewrite a deleted record, the linked list chain of deleted records is broken. It could be worse than that. The data values that you may have in your record could be interpreted by the software as a linked list ADDR pointer and strange results can occur. It is safer to always know where you are and not write over a deleted record.

It would be possible for the toolset functions to enforce what is suggested above. Put_record could test every record being written to see if it has been deleted. The delete flag in the record would provide that information. That test was intentionally omitted to avoid the overhead cost. Each rewrite of a record would involve a routine read of whatever is in that record's space. Being in control of the code that decides what record to write, the programmer avoids the violation. If it happens, it is a bug in the program, to be revealed during testing. Things don't always work out that way, and if it worries you, then install some defensive code into put_record and pay the price. So far, this has never been a problem.

```
int rcd_length (fd)
int fd;
```

This function returns the length of the record associated with the file specified by **fd**. If the file is not open, ERROR is returned.

Summary

With the completion of this chapter, we have a small set of subroutines, a way to drive our keyboard and screen, a technique for the management of random data buffers, and a file management subsystem to get data to and from random files in a consistent and easy-to-use manner. These are the cornerstones of an interactive system. Using these, we could write individual programs to interactively store and retrieve data in an on-line environment.

In Chapter 8, I introduce the concept of an executive program that integrates all of the processes with a standard system of menus.

Menu
Management

This chapter presents the menu management subsystem. These functions provide for the control of execution of interactive application programs through the use of a table-driven menu executive process. You must make a clear distinction between menus and data entry screens. The menu, which is the subject of this chapter, and the data entry screen, which is the subject of Chapter 9, have only one thing in common; they both use the keyboard and screen. But there is a difference; menus control the execution of programs, and data entry screens manage the collection of input data. The strength of the menu management subsystem is in the rigid set of standard display techniques with which a system must conform. Conversely, the strength of the screen management subsystem (Chapter 9) is the flexibility it allows in the formats and contents of data entry screens.

A menu is a list of options that is displayed on the screen and from which the user may select a process. The menu lists the processes by using descriptive words that are meaningful to the user. Then, by keying in a code that is associated on the menu with the desired function, the user selects a process, and the computer executes it. Figure 8-1 is an example of a menu.

A menu consists of three basic components. First is the title of the menu. This is usually associated with the process that the user is considering when the menu is displayed. Second is a list of selections. These are the choices provided on the menu for the user. The final menu component provides a way for the user to make a selection.

Menu selections can take one of several forms. In the example of

```
┌──────────────────────────────────────────────┐
│                                                │
│        MEMBERSHIP  MAINTENANCE  MENU           │
│                                                │
│     1. Add A Membership Record                 │
│     2. Change An Existing Membership Record    │
│     3. Delete A Membership Record              │
│     ESC to return to Main Menu                 │
│                                                │
│     Enter Selection [__]                       │
│                                                │
└──────────────────────────────────────────────┘
```

Figure 8-1. A menu.

Figure 8-1 the selections are numbered, and the user selects one by keying the number associated with the selection. Another technique allows the user to press an alphabetic key associated with a word in the selection. Here is an example of that:

A-dd

C-hange

D-elete

The user would type A, C, or D to make a choice. This limits the menu to selections beginning with unique letters. The menu management software supports this kind of menu. A third technique uses special function keys on the keyboard. The IBM PC keyboard has 10 function keys labeled F1 through F10. The software also supports function keys.

Other techniques that are popular use light pens, joysticks, touch panels, digitizers, track balls, and mice to allow the user to make a selection. These require special hardware not found in all personal computers. We do not use any of these in our menu management functions because we do not want to limit ourselves to any specific configuration of hardware.

Keep in mind, however, that if you are developing a system where one or more of these devices are available, you should probably try to use them.

The toolset uses menus like the one in Figure 8-1. The menus and their selections are described in an array of structures, which defines the text of each menu and the actions to be taken as the result of user selections. The menu management functions cause those actions to be taken.

There are two categories of selections. First is the selection made by a user who is viewing a menu. Second is a value returned by an applications function or program. This looks just like a user selection to the menu management software and causes actions to be taken accordingly. A user selection is called a "selection," and a function selection is called a "soft selection." A selection must actually appear on the visible menu to be valid, but a soft selection need only be described in the array of menu-defining structures. The purpose of the soft selection is to allow applications software to influence the flow of processing as the result of internal decisions based upon data other than user selections.

There are three kinds of actions. First, a menu selection can cause another menu to become effective. The current effective menu is called the "menu-in-force." Second, a menu selection can cause execution of an application function or program. Finally, selection of the ESCAPE key causes the system to retreat to the menu that was in force immediately prior to the current one. If the current menu is the first one, the ESCAPE key terminates execution of the menu functions.

What is the use of all this? Its purpose is twofold. First, it eliminates a lot of redundant executive code in the application programs. With this capability you can concentrate on the code that solves your particular problem at hand. You can write functions that deal with the requirements of your user and let the toolset handle the requirements of the system. This supports our objectives for information hiding discussed in the chapter called "Software Development Philosophy."

The second purpose for this subsystem is that it provides a measure of uniformity in the user interface. A lot has been written on the subject of human–machine interface. (You can usually find a human factors expert at any water cooler or cocktail party. They are easy to spot. They say "user friendly" a lot.) It is generally accepted that consistency in the language between the user and the machine is desirable. Not that your language wouldn't have consistency if you wrote all the code yourself. But, by using the the toolset, you have it without trying.

Let's look at what the menu management functions provide. Once the executive structure has been described to the functions, the functions display the menus and manage the software execution. When a user has made a selection that calls for the execution of a process, the menu manager executes it. This is done by using one of the two methods, function calling or program fetching.

Function calling is the call, by the menu manager, of an application function by using the function pointer mechanism of C. Program fetching is the load and execute of an independently compiled C program. Most C compilers allow a program to fetch other programs. The new program returns to the original program when processing is complete.

It could be suggested that overlays are an appropriate way to manage application software execution. Many C compilers implement an overlay scheme, but there is no standard way to do it. One of the compilers used to develop the toolset functions supports overlays, and their use was tempting. But, without that compiler, you would have to make significant changes to the tools so the use of overlays was abandoned.

The menu manager is restricted to the two methods just mentioned. An implementation that does not include the fetching capability must be limited to the function-calling method. This means that all of the code for the application will be linked together into one executable module.

If a program tries to use the program fetch in a system that doesn't support it, the menu management function displays a fatal error message and terminates the program.

Let's take a look at how the executive works. It acts upon the concept of a two-dimensional array of menus and selections as illustrated in Figure 8-2. The columns of the array are menus-in-force. The rows are selections. The elements of the array contain actions for the executive to take when a selection (or a soft selection) is made for a menu.

The user's typed selection or the soft selection from a previously called program is converted to an integer from 1 to the highest selection value allowed. This selection is used to form an intersection with the menu-in-force vector in the array of menus and selections to extract another element and execute another action. In Figure 8-2, the menu-in-force is 2, and the selection being shown is 3. At the intersection of these two vectors in the matrix is the "action" to be taken.

The actions are either new menu-in-force vectors, pointers to functions to be executed or names of programs to be fetched. If the action is a menu vector, the indicated menu is displayed and becomes the new menu-in-force, and the software waits for a user selection. If the action from the array element is a function

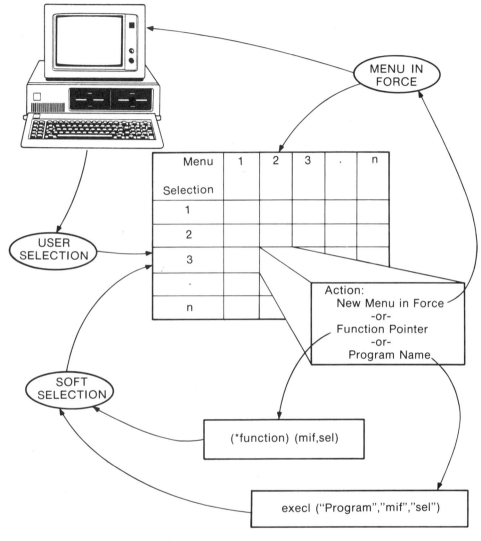

Figure 8-2.

pointer, the function is called and is expected to return a soft selection. If the action is a program name, that program is fetched, and it is expected to return a soft selection in the completion code.

If a function or fetched program returns zero for a soft selection, the current menu-in-force is redisplayed, and the user must make a selection.

The design of the executive architecture of the system cannot be taken lightly. First comes the development of a hierarchy of menus and functions followed by an array of menu structures that describe the menu architecture to the menu management functions. Figure 8-3 is a chart showing the relationship between menus and processes in a simple membership accounting system. The unshadowed boxes are menus; the shadowed boxes are processes that are executed as the result of selections from menus.

The implementation of a menu strategy such as the one in Figure 8-3 involves the development of a C program that contains an array of initialized structures describing each menu and the nature of the selections. The program should include "menu.h" because the structure is defined there. Here is what the structure looks like.

```
struct mif    {
    char *m_title;            /* menu title                  */
    char *keytab;             /* pointer to keystroke table */
    struct    {               /* actions                     */
        char *m_sel;          /* text of selection           */
        int m_vector;         /* vector to new menu          */
        int (*func) ();       /* pointer to function         */
        char *pname;          /* name of program to fetch    */
        } sels [MXSELS];      /* one action per selection    */
};
```

Remember that this is an array of structures, one entry in the array for each menu in the system. If the system has three menus each having two selections, the structure might look like the one shown in the program "smalmenu.c" (Listing 8-1).

Initialization of the structure array should be done in such a way that the menus can be easily read. Initialized structures in C can be confusing if you don't make orderly use of white space (blanks, tabs, newlines) to make the source code legible.

Following is a discussion of each of the fields in the structure. Read this along with the listing of menu.h and the initialized structure in menuexmp.c in this chapter.

The character array called **m_title** contains the name of the menu. This name appears at the top of the screen when the menu is displayed.

The character pointer named **keytab** points to a table that describes the keystrokes needed for each menu selection. If func-

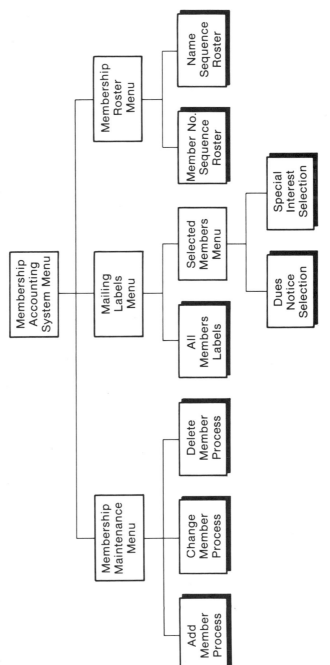

Figure 8-3. Relationship between menus and processes in a simple membership accounting system.

```
/* ---------------- smalmenu.c ---------------- */

#include "toolset.h"
#include "menu.h"
main()
{
    static struct mif mn [] = {
        {"menu 1", 0, {{"1 = menu 2", 2,    0,    ""},
                       {"2 = menu 3", 3,    0,    ""}}},
        {"menu 2", 0, {{"1 = menu 1", 1,    0,    ""},
                       {"2 = menu 3", 3,    0,    ""}}},
        {"menu 3", 0, {{"1 = menu 1", 1,    0,    ""},
                       {"2 = menu 2", 2,    0,    ""}}}
    };
    menu_exec(mn, 1, 0, 0);
}
```

Listing 8-1.

tion keys or alphabetic letters are not used for selections, put a
null pointer in the keytab member of the structure. The software
then defaults to the digits 1, 2, and so on. The table works as follows: The first entry in the table is the value to be used for the
first selection on the menu, the second is for the second, and so
on. The sample program "menuexmp.c" (Listing 8-2) shows how
to use this table.

```
/* -------------------- menuexmp.c -------------------------- */

#include <stdio.h>
#include "toolset.h"
#include "screen.h"
#include "keys.h"
#include "menu.h"
int banner(), notimpl();

main()
{
    static char keytab [] = {F1, F2, F3};       /* Function keys          */
    static char alphtab [] = {'a', 's'};        /* Keystrokes for Menu 2  */
    static struct mif mf [] = {
    {"Main Menu", keytab,
        {{"F1 = Membership Maintenance",      0,    0,        "example.exe"},
         {"F2 = Mailing Labels",              2,    0,        ""},
         {"F3 = Membership Roster",           3,    0,        ""}}},
    {"Mailing Labels", alphtab,
        {{"A-11 members",                     0,    notimpl,  ""},
         {"S-elected members",               4,    0,        ""}}},
    {"Membership Roster", keytab,
        {{"F1 = Membership Number Sequence", 0,    notimpl,  ""},
         {"F2 = Member Name Sequence",        0,    0,        "sortexmp.exe"}}},
    {"Mailing Labels, Selected Members", 0,
        {{"1 = Dues Notice Selection",       0,    notimpl,  ""},
         {"2 = Special Interest Selection",  0,    notimpl,  ""}}}
```

Listing 8-2.

Listing 8-2 (continued)

```
};
int minf = 1, sel = 0;
```

```
nner);
```

```
anner writer ------------- */
```

```
UNTING SYSTEM ))");
```

```
ion ------------------ */
```

```
.");
```

ITEM CHARGED

Patron: Qiufang Tian
Patron Barcode: 60179600190
Patron Group: Graduate Stuc

Due Date: 2/21/98 20:00

Title: C developmer
Author: Stevens, Al, 1
Item Barcode: 39346005622

ructure is an array of structures that includes an
selection on the menu. First is a character array
at contains the text that is displayed on the screen
of the selections. Next are three mutually exclu-
describe the action. Only one of these fields may
he other two must be null. The integer **m_vector**
ber relative to one that indicates that the selection
ferent menu to be executed. The function pointer
d with a pointer to a function to be executed by
the selection. The character array **pname** is the name of an exter-
nally compiled program that is not linked with the executive software but that is to be executed when the selection is made.

With the structure initialized as required, the application program calls the function **menu_exec** (described later). Of course,
provision must be made for the functions and programs named in
the structure to be executed by **menu_exec.**

Looking back at the program "smalmenu.c," you can gain in-
sight into how the menu management functions handle the hierarchy of the menus-in-force. The program implements three
menus, each one having two selections. Each selection on a menu
causes one of the other two menus to become the new menu-in-
force. This apparent dead loop continues until you use ESCAPE
to terminate the program.

The program "menuexmp.c" (Listing 8-2), is a more complex and realistic example of the use of the menu management software. It doesn't really do anything other than navigate throughout a menu structure similar to that in Figure 8-3, but, it is similar to menu management programs that are written for real applications. In addition to the menu-in-force swaps of "smalmenu.c," it also illustrates the calling of a simulated application function and the fetching of two of our other example programs, "sortexmp.c" and "example.c," which can be found in Chapters 10 and 12, respectively.

Menu Function

Only one function in the menu management software is called by the application software. To use it, include the following statements in your calling program:

```
#include <toolset.h>
#include <menu.h>
```

```
menu_exec (mp, mf, sel, banner)
struct mif *mp;
int mf, sel;
int (*banner) ();
```

This function is called with an initialized structure array of type mif. The pointer mp points to the structure array. Menu_exec does not care how many elements are in the array. It depends upon the menu vectors in the array to point to valid menus. In the array, the menus are numbered relative to 1. See "menuexmp.c" (Listing 8-2) for an example of how this is done. Menu_exec usually begins by displaying the menu indicated by mf and getting a selection from the user. A menu number in the vectors that is greater than the number of defined menus will cause menu_exec to get lost.

The integers mf and sel tell the function where to start in the table of menus. The starting menu-in-force is in mf. It is a number relative to 1 that identifies the first menu to be executed. The integer sel is a soft selection. If it has a zero value, the menu is displayed and a user selection is required to get things underway. If it has any other value, it is assumed to be a soft selection, and the corresponding action is executed from the specified menu without user intervention.

The function considers the array as representing a hierarchical menu structure with menu 1 at the top of the hierarchy. If it starts at any menu other than 1, the logical path back to menu 1 is not known by the function. Therefore, the function begins by assuming that menu 1 is immediately ahead of whatever menu it started with. After that, it can chart the user's navigation through the menus as allowed by the table entries.

The function pointer named **banner** allows menus to be customized. If you don't need to use the feature, send a null (0) in place of the pointer. (When sending nulls for pointers, use a cast; in some compilers the pointer length is different than the integer length.) To use the feature, send a pointer to a function that is to be executed when each menu is displayed. The function will be called after the screen is cleared and before the menu is displayed. The function can write a banner line, borders, logo or anything else to customize the menus, and need not return anything. The banner function is called everytime any menu is displayed. It allows you to add a personal touch of consistency to the menus, perhaps by using the graphics features of your machine.

In displaying custom data, try to avoid the upper left corner of the screen. This is where the error message is shown when the user enters an invalid selection. It uses the first 17 columns of the first row on the screen. The menu display software vertically centers the menu on the screen. It uses the global definitions, HEIGHT and WIDTH to determine the screen row and column dimensions, and builds a menu consisting of the title, a blank line, the selection text lines, another blank line and the Enter Selection line. The title is horizontally centered, and, on a 24 × 80 screen, the selections begin at column 21 and the Enter Selection line begins at column 24.

Summary

With the implementation of the functions in this chapter, we can build interactive systems with a common user interface for program execution. Because the program executions are independent of our menu process, we have hidden a complex part of our software system inside of our tools. We will carry the concept a step further in the next chapter with complex data entry screens and a package of reusable software that totally manages the interactive entry of data to our system.

Data
Screen
Management

⑨

In the last chapter we implemented automatic menu control in a set of functions primarily concerned with menus as screen displays. From a table that described the menus and the application program execution logic, the software displayed menus, got selections from the user, and properly executed the applications functions. In this chapter we are concerned with a more complex kind of screen display called "data entry screens." The formats for these displays vary widely depending upon the requirements of the application, and the data that the user enters is more complex than simple menu selections.

A menu (as implemented in Chapter 8) has only one data element, the user selection, and it has a standard format for display of the text of the selections. On the other hand, data entry screens can be designed in any of many formats by using a wide range of display techniques. The requirements for data entry are much more diverse than those of the menu. The power of the menu is in the matrix of command vectors and pointers that underpins it and its ability to manage the execution of programs by using complex hierarchical logic. The data entry screen needs none of that.

A menu is a simple entry of data which controls a complex piece of logic; a data entry screen manages the complex entry of complex data. The data entry process is not integral to the executive processes of menu management and, therefore, need not be integrated with the menu software; the menu does not require the overhead of complex data screen management.

The environment supported by the software in the toolset is one where the system user looks at a video screen and types on a keyboard. The screen provides information about what the user is expected to type and displays the results of what the computer does with it. This is called the interactive environment because the user interacts with the computer by using the keyboard and screen as the medium for data exchange.

A lot about this kind of user interface is common from application to application. One can capitalize on this commonality by having a set of screen management software functions that can be used over and over. These are a valuable addition to a software tool collection and are further evidence of the wisdom of the tool building concept.

The screen management software does a lot of what the block mode terminal does. A block mode terminal reads blocks of data from the computer and displays it based upon a template description of what is meant to be input data and what is meant to be output data. The user enters data onto the screen into input areas and cannot enter data where the screen template has areas defined as output. These templates are controlled by the terminal; the computer is not communicating with the terminal while data entry is going on. When the user keys a special "enter" code, the terminal transmits all of the input data to the computer in one block. The computer processes the data as a record, and the iteration repeats.

Given the availability of inexpensive block mode terminals, why is software needed to make a dumb terminal look smart? Why not just get some smart ones? First let's consider the environment in which this software should be used. We are not developing a system that supports a large number of simultaneous on-line users connected to a host main frame. This is interactive software for a personal computer, and there are four good reasons for having the screen management subsytem.

The first reason relates to the hardware configuration of many personal computers. The configuration does not use terminals; it uses an integrated keyboard and video memory. It is addressed as a terminal in most applications code, but it doesn't have block mode terminal features like field protect and automatic editing. Of course, this isn't the case with all PCs, but the integrated keyboard and screen have become a dominant hardware architecture, and almost all new systems are being built that way. We want our software to run with terminals, but we also want to run it on the PCs.

The second reason addresses the desire to develop portable code. There is no accepted standard for the protocols of a block mode terminal. There is a proposed standard (ANSI 3.64), but it is not widely embraced by the terminal industry. The situation is so extreme that recent generation terminals feature the ability to emulate earlier popular terminals in an attempt to capture a follow-on market for terminals. Some terminals can emulate several others. You might find yourself developing software for a system where the target terminal is not yet known. Often the terminal configuration is changed in the middle of a task, or there are several kinds of them. It is extremely difficult to exploit the characteristics of an unknown configuration. The tendency here is to develop software that intentionally avoids certain desirable features because it is not evident that they will be available.

The third reason for using this software has to do with the human factors that should be built into a system. The system should provide on-line help when the user needs it and should give diagnostic messages as soon as the user makes an error. During the entry of data, the user should be able to press a "help" function key and receive custom help information right away. The system should not wait for the screen entry to be completed and transmitted in block mode to learn that the user needs help with one of the fields on the screen. Besides, when the user enters a data value, the applications software system should have the opportunity to validate it at once rather than after the entire screen is filled out.

The last reason is the most important one. If we don't develop and use software tools, then we must invent the same wheel every time we design and code a new interactive system. The requirements for screen management are so alike from system to system that they are a natural for the tool building concept. It is folly to rewrite the same logic in each new project, and it is tiresome to have to solve the same problems again and again. Our attention is better directed to the unique requirements of the application. Wherever possible, software should be written to be reusable.

The Top–Down Approach to Screen Management

Use of the screen management functions consists of building display formats and the automated interfaces to them. A very basic approach to this work involves these four steps:

1. A word processor or text editor (the same software used to build source code) is used to build screen images. This results in a file that contains templates of the screens used by the toolset functions to manage data entry.
2. Tables are defined that are internal to the application program and that describe the characteristics of each screen in terms of the data elements that appear on it.
3. Functions are developed to provide data validation and user help.
4. The application program is developed to process the data entered by the user on the screen.

This is the top–down approach. It starts with the user interface as expressed in the screen format. Then the format is described in a lower-level coded table. Finally, code is written that passes the tabular screen description to the screen manager, and the manager collects the data.

Screen Design

A "screen" in our discussion is a single display on a video screen surface. It consists of a collection of data elements and, optionally, some textual information that is of interest to the user who enters data onto the screen. Figures 9-1 and 9-2 are examples of screens. Figure 9-1 illustrates a typical data entry screen. The user observes the contents of a record from the data base and, optionally, enters some changes to it. In this example, the data elements are from an employee file record. Figure 9-2 shows the kind of screen used to collect routine transactions for the posting of entries. This figure shows how a time accounting system might use data entry to collect hours expended against labor accounts. These are two different kinds of data entry procedures, either of which could be implemented by using the screen management subsystem in our toolset.

The principles of screen design are a subject of much discussion and controversy. Everyone is a screen designer. If you are involved in a project where the screen designs are subject to anyone's review, you will find this to be true. Prepare to change your

```
+--------------------------------------------------------------+
|              WEEKLY TIME CARD ENTRY                          |
|                                                              |
|  Week Ending:    __/__/__                                    |
|                                                              |
|  Employee #:             _____                          |
|                                                              |
|                 ----------------Hours Worked----------------  |
|  Charge #       Sun   Mon   Tue   Wed   Thu   Fri   Sat      |
|  _____      __    __    __    __    __    __    __       |
|  _____      __    __    __    __    __    __    __       |
|  _____      __    __    __    __    __    __    __       |
|  _____      __    __    __    __    __    __    __       |
|  _____      __    __    __    __    __    __    __       |
+--------------------------------------------------------------+
```

Figure 9-1. A data entry screen.

```
+--------------------------------------------------------------+
|          PERSONNEL FILE MAINTENANCE ENTRY SCREEN            |
|                                                              |
|  Employee #:          _____                             |
|                                                              |
|  Employee Name:  _____            |
|  Address:        _____            |
|                  _____            |
|  City:           _____            |
|  State/Zip:      __      _____                          |
|                                                              |
|  Date Hired:     __/__/__      Hourly Wage:    $__.__        |
|  SSN:            __-__-____                                  |
|                                                              |
|  Dept. #:        _____                                  |
+--------------------------------------------------------------+
```

Figure 9-2. The screen used to collect routine
transactions for the posting of entries.

design several times before you are done, and submit your screen designs for approval well before any other substantive work is underway that depends upon them. There is always plenty of guidance after most of the work is done, but in the end it is up to you, the system designer, to apply some informed understanding of the task at hand. This is a cooperative effort between you and the user. Your knowledge of systems and the user's understanding of the application should complement each other. Usually, neither of you knows enough about both to claim supremacy in the great screen debate.

Building a Screen Definition

Screen design uses a screen or text editor. Actually, a screen editor is better than the typical line editor program because it allows you to see the screen during design as it appears to the user when the system is running. All of the screens for a given interactive program are built into one file because the software reads them into a buffer and collects data with this copy of the screens.

These are the rules for screen design.

1. Place an asterisk (*) at the beginning of each screen. The asterisk identifies to the software the beginning of each screen image in the file.

2. Do not use the asterisk for anything else in the screen. If this is not acceptable, use some other special character for screen separation in your file, and modify the software to recognize it in place of the asterisk. The global symbol SCRNID defines this character.

3. Use the underline character (__) to define screen data elements. I call it the "field filler character." Do not use the underline for anything else. Each data element on the screen is represented by a string of underlines, and the length of each element is determined by the number of underlines. As with the asterisk, there is a global symbol, named FLDFILL, to define the field filler character. If the underline is needed for other reasons, pick a different field filler character and change the definition of FLDFILL.

4. The following punctuation characters may be used inside of a string of underlines: period, comma, either parenthesis, hyphen, slash, or colon. For example, here are two data elements, a date and a telephone number with area code.

> Date: __/__/__ Phone: (____)____-_____

The punctuation characters are not a part of the collected data, and do not count in the length of the data element. The date just shown has a length of 6 bytes, and the phone number has a length of 10 bytes. Do not try to use a space for punctuation. The program considers the space as separation between data elements. A currency field can be described like this:

> Amount: $__,____.____

The dollar sign and comma are not required, and there can be as many underlines to the right of the decimal as you wish.

5. Place text wherever it is needed throughout the screen. Just be sure not to use the asterisk or underline in it.

6. Tabs, carriage returns, and line feeds may be used to represent white space in the screen. The asterisk that identifies the next screen or, if there is no next screen, the end-of-file, causes the remainder of the screen to be blank.

7. Leave the top line blank. The screen software uses it for notices, error messages, and the <INSERT> toggle message. If data must be on the top line, don't use positions 1-50 or 56-71. Messages and the toggle are displayed in those positions, and anything else you put there will be overwritten.

A screen file, when built, looks exactly like the screen images it represents with an asterisk at the beginning of each screen image. Figure 9-3 shows the contents of the screen file to describe the screens in Figures 9-1 and 9-2.

Screen Tables

To describe the data entry system to the screen management functions, develop a program that describes each screen and the data fields on each. The program calls the functions to collect the data and provides collection buffers, validation functions, and help functions. This description is passed to the screen processing software in the form of a pointer to a structure, the definition of which is known to both the calling and called functions. The structure is named scrn__buf; its format is found in "screen.h" in Appendix A. There is an array of structures for each different screen template in the system. Each structure element in the array represents one field on the screen. Following is a list of the values placed in the structure members.

1. An indicator giving the type of the data element. Elements can be of type currency (C), alphanumeric (A) or date (D). Numeric data elements are further defined as zero-filled (Z) or space-filled (N); both are right-justified. Alphanumeric fields are always left-justified and can accept any printable ASCII character during data entry. Dates are left-justified numeric entries, and must pass a date validation when entered.

Line #	Data
01	*
02	PERSONEL FILE MAINTENANCE ENTRY SCREEN
03	
04	Employee #: _____
05	
06	Employee Name: _____
07	Address: _____
08	_____
09	City: _____
10	State/Zip: ___ _____
11	
12	Date Hired: ___/___/___ Hourly Wage: $___.___
13	SSN: ___-___-___
14	
15	Dept. #: _____
16	*
17	WEEKLY TIME CARD ENTRY
18	
19	Week Ending: ___/___/___
20	
21	Employee #: _____
22	
23	_____Hours Worked_____
24	Charge # Sun Mon Tue Wed Thu Fri Sat
25	_____ __ __ __ __ __ __ __
26	_____ __ __ __ __ __ __ __
27	_____ __ __ __ __ __ __ __
28	_____ __ __ __ __ __ __ __
29	_____ __ __ __ __ __ __ __
30	

Figure 9-3. The contents of the screen file that describes the screens in Figures 9-1 and 9-2.

2. A true/false indicator telling if the element is write-protected. When this indicator is true, the user may not overtype the data.

3. A pointer to a character array where the screen software is to collect data for this element. The length of the character array must be equal to one plus the length of the screen element as defined by the number of underlines in the screen definition. The extra position is for a null string terminator. So, if there is a date data element with six underlines in the screen definition (__/__/__), then the array must have seven characters in it. If the pointer points to this array:

```
char today [7];
```

then, after data entry, the array contains six ASCII digits of date (two for day, two for month and two for year) followed by the null ('\0') string terminator.

4. Pointers to custom coded functions for editing or otherwise processing the data element when it is first entered and for providing help to the user when the HELP function key is pressed with the cursor in the data element in question. These pointers must be NULL if no functions are to be called.

5. A true/false indicator telling the software to automatically fill the data element on the screen with data from the caller's collection space when the screen is first displayed.

6. A true/false indicator telling if an automatic DITTO is desired when the screen is first displayed. This key causes the element to duplicate the previous value from the previous copy of the screen.

7. A pointer to a character array to save previous data element values for the ditto functions.

Data Entry

Data entry occurs when the applications function calls the scrn__proc function after the file of screen templates and the scrn__buf structure have been properly initialized. The scrn__proc function does quite a lot. There are standard features such as help processing, data validation, and options based upon entries in the calling function's scrn__buf structure.

The function displays the screen template and places the cursor into the first field on the screen. The user keys data, and the function collects it into the caller's data buffer, providing help, validation, and general data entry support.

During the user's data entry, the software controls the cursor location with respect to the data entry fields on the template. The cursor is kept inside of the areas where data fields are to be entered. If the user fills a field, the cursor automatically advances to the next one. The cursor control arrow keys operate as they should, moving the cursor backward and forward and moving from field to field when the end of a field is encountered. The cursor down and up arrows move the cursor out of its current field to the closest field on the next lower or higher line on the screen. The TAB and Return keys advance the cursor to the next field.

Any time the cursor is moved out of a field, the caller-supplied edit function associated with that field is called.

Function keys are available for the deletion of single characters directly under and directly to the left of the cursor. These keys cause the appropriate shifting of data to the right of the cursor within the data element being processed. As published, the Backspace key on the IBM PC keyboard deletes the character to the left of the cursor, and the Del key deletes the one to the right.

The user can select the insert mode by using the INSERT key. On the IBM PC, the Ins key is used for the insert mode. When the mode is entered, the token <INSERT> is displayed at the top of the screen. Then, as the user types new characters, those to the right of the cursor in the current field are shifted one character position to the right. The last character of the data element is truncated. The INSERT key is used to turn the insert mode off as well as on.

A field can be specified as being write-protected. Such a field is bypassed by the software when the cursor is being moved around the screen. This field is useful when a template has data elements that provide information to the user but are not to be modified by the current transaction.

Screen Data Initialization

A field can be initially displayed with data already in the data collection buffer, or the collection buffer can be cleared prior to data entry. The first option allows the application to load the collection area with data from, for example, a file record and then to have the screen manager display it and collect changes to it. The second option allows for the data to be initialized with blanks each time a new transaction is begun. There can be a mix of these options among fields on the same screen.

The DITTO Key

Scrn__proc handles DITTO processing on a field-by-field basis. For any field, it can be specified that when the user presses the DITTO function key, the previous entry value is copied to the current field and displayed. A field can also be automatically copied from its previous value when the screen is first displayed. This process can be handy when a data element frequently has the same value from transaction to transaction. Examples might be the posting date, the state a customer lives in, or a voucher number. To use the DITTO key or the automatic copy feature, the caller provides a buffer to hold the data element value from the previous screen and a pointer to the buffer. The pointer is placed in the scrn_buf structure; the buffer is wherever it can be conveniently placed.

Entry Help Processing

Don't always expect the user to know exactly what to enter, even though the screen template contains all sorts of helpful prompting information. For those data elements where additional help is needed, a custom help function can be coded that is automatically called when the HELP function key is pressed. A help function should be declared as one that returns a character pointer. The help function may use any of the screen area for any purpose (a list of possible entries, for example) and may even provide a data value for the data element by returning a pointer to a character array. If no value is to be returned, the help function should return a pointer to a null string. Be sure and make the distinction between the pointer to a null string and a null pointer.

Wrong:

```
return (char *) NULL; /* NULL char ptr   */
```

Right:

```
return " ";            /* ptr to NULL str */
```

Usually, a help function displays a tutorial body of text that explains to the user what is required for the current data element. But, when the data element must match a value in a table, then the table can be displayed on the screen to allow the user to select from the displayed table entries and then return a pointer to the entry that was selected. This is code that the caller must provide; but, the screen manager has the exit points during data entry to allow it.

Data Validation

The software performs primitive validation or editing of the data as it is entered. (I am using the term "edit" in the data processing sense. To edit data is to test it for valid content.) Numeric data must be a valid digit, 0-9. A date must have a valid month and day. Unrecognized control characters are rejected. Each rejected input causes an appropriate error message to be displayed at the top of the screen, and the cursor remains in the offending data element. Any further edits become the responsibility of the application software. Applications functions to edit data elements are identified in the scrn__buf structure. A pointer to the function is included in the scrn__buf structure, and the function is called by scrn__proc when the data element has been entered by the user. The screen management functions declare and call the caller__defined edit function like this:

```
int (*edit_funct) ();    /* a function pointer   */
char *data_ptr;          /* -> the entered data  */
char term_byte;          /* the entry terminator */
int edit_result;         /* what the edit returns */
    .
    .
    .
/* the function pointer you pass is put into edit_funct */
    .
edit_result = (*edit_funct) (data_ptr, term_byte);
```

The edit function that you code should expect **data_ptr** to point to a character array containing the data to be edited and a null terminating byte. The character variable term__byte contains the keystroke that terminated entry of the data (for example, '\n'). You must code the function to return ERROR or OK depending upon the validity of the data. OK allows the screen processing to proceed with the next data element on the screen. An ERROR return causes the cursor to remain on the current data element. Prior to returning ERROR, **err_msg** can be called with an appropriate message. This puts the message at the top of the screen and sounds the computer's audible alarm. An edit function for a single character field that must be 'Y' or 'N' might be coded like this:

```
int edit_yn (data_ptr, term_byte)
char *data_ptr;
char term_byte;
{
    if (*data_ptr != 'Y' && *data_ptr != 'N') {
        err_msg ("Y or N only");
        return ERROR;
    }
    return OK;
}
```

Completion of Data Entry

There are three ways for data entry on a template to be considered complete. The first way requires that the GO key be pressed to complete the entry. The second way completes the entry when the data value for the last field is entered. Finally, if the user presses a function key or the ESCAPE key at any time, data entry is terminated. The keystroke that ended the entry is returned to the calling function.

There is good reason for the differences in the first two approaches. In the view of the user, there is more than one kind of data entry screen. In the case where the user is casually browsing the data base, updating existing records or adding records, and where the screen has many data elements, the user may wish to move the cursor around the fields on the screen, changing them and rechanging them. Then, when the user is satisfied with the screen, he or she presses the GO function key to complete the entry. In a different situation, the user might be entering routine transactions, as in the point-of-sale entry of stock number and quantity. No browsing is desired or necessary. When the last data element is entered on the screen, the data collection is considered complete. Figure 9-1 is typical of the former kind of screen; Figure 9-2 might be the latter.

It is up to the caller to react properly to how data entry was completed on a particular screen, regardless of which of the three ways is used. The ESCAPE key might be used to terminate the data entry program; function keys might be used to page forward or backward or to delete a record; the GO key might be used to cause an entered record to be written to the data base. For a given record entry, any of these values might be returned, and the calling program must react appropriately.

Screen Management Global Definitions

The screen management functions described here assume the assignment of values to a number of global definitions. These are maintained in the source file "screen.h." The file "keys.h" contains global definitions that provide the values for the keystrokes. These vary depending upon which terminal or personal computer is used. Values coded in "keys.h" are ones that are used for the IBM PC.

An Example of Screen Management

Here is a simple screen that allows a user to type the time and date into the computer.

```
*
Time: __:__:__
Date: __/__/__
```

The asterisk identifies the beginning of the screen. There are two data elements on the screen, the time and the date. The colons in the time and the slashes in the date are punctuation characters. Assume that this description is in a file named "dttim.crt." Listing 9-1 is a program to process that file.

```
/* ---------------------- dattim.c ------------------------------ */

#include (stdio.h)
#include "toolset.h"
#include "screen.h"
#include "keys.h"

#define et(cc) (((*cc-'0')*10)+(*(cc+1)-'0'))

/* cannot use Lattice or DeSmet C Compiler with this program */
/* because long form of bdos function is required */

struct { char hr [2], mi [2], se [3]; } tm;      /* time data */
struct { char mo [2], da [2], yr [3]; } dt;      /* date data */
struct scrn_buf dtm [] = {                        /* screen definition table */
    { 'Z', FALSE, (char *) &tm, 0, 0, FALSE, FALSE, 0 },/* time */
    { 'D', FALSE, (char *) &dt, 0, 0, FALSE, FALSE, 0 } /* date */
};

main()
{
    read_screens("dttim.crt");
    if (scrn_proc(1, dtm, TRUE) != ESC) {
        bdos(45, et(tm.se)*256, et(tm.hr)*256 + et(tm.mi));
        bdos(43, et(dt.mo)*256 + et(dt.da), et(dt.yr) + 1900);
    }
    reset_screens();
}
```

Listing 9-1.

The Dattim program includes the files "toolset.h," "screen.h," and "keys.h," which make all of the global definitions needed for screen management. Values that the user enters are stored in the structures **tm** and **dt**, and the **dtm** structure is the screen definition. Three screen management functions are called by this program; **read_screens** is called to initialize the system with the screen template file named "dttim.crt," **scrn_proc** is called to read the data from the keyboard, and `reset_screens` closes out the program's use of the screen management functions. These functions are explained in greater detail in the next section. There are other screen management functions that a caller might use. These are described in the next section, and examples of their use can be found in the program "example.c" in Chapter 12.

The function named **bdos** is taken from the Aztec C86 library of system-dependent functions for MS-DOS and PC-DOS. The **#define** macro named **et** converts two adjacent ASCII numeric characters into an integer for the **bdos** function calls. It converts the two-character components of time (hours, minutes, seconds) and of the date (year, month, day) into integers. These are converted to the **bdos** function call conventions for 8088 register parameters.

Dattim.c is not a portable program in that it is specific to the MS-DOS operating system and can only be compiled with the Aztec C86 compiler. Its purpose here is to illustrate the use of the screen management functions.

Screen Functions

These functions support screen processing and are called by the application software.

```
VOID read_screens (screen_name)
char *screen_name;
```

This function is called before data entry begins. Its purpose is to read the screen templates from its disk file and prepare the templates for subsequent use. The character pointer `screen_name` points to a character array containing the template file name. If no such file exists, the function displays a fatal error message and terminates the program.

```
char scrn_proc (scrn_no, scrn_data, go_last)
int scrn_no;
struct scrn_buf *scrn_data;
int go_last;
```

This function is called by the application program to collect data into memory with the screen and the keyboard. The first parameter to the function identifies the screen number. If several screen templates are in the screen file, the first one is screen 1, the second is screen 2, and so on.

The second parameter is a pointer to the structure array that describes the screen. The array of structures is of type `scrn_buf` and has one entry per field on the screen. The call to this function points to the first entry in the array. Members of the structure describe the characteristics of the field as they relate to data entry. The structure also provides a pointer to the data collection buffer provided by the calling function.

The `go_last` parameter is either TRUE or FALSE to indicate whether the user's entry of data on the screen is to be completed by the GO function key or following entry of data for the last field on the screen. Regardless of which method is used, completion of data entry causes this function to return to the calling function.

When the screen data collection is over, the function returns the keystroke that terminated it. This can be the ESC key, the GO key, the carriage return, a function key or a null byte ('\0'), indicating that the last data element on the template was entered with the `go_last` parameter set to FALSE.

```
VOID err_msg (s)
char *s;
```

This function posts an error message on the message line and sounds the audible alarm. The character pointer s points to a null terminated string that should be no longer than 50 characters.

```
VOID notice (s)
char *s;
```

This function is similar to err__msg except that the message is a notice rather than an alert. The difference is that the audible alarm is not sounded and the notice is displayed at half intensity.

```
VOID clrmsg ()
```

This function clears the error message line.

```
VOID backfill (scrn_no, item, screen_data)
int scrn_no;
int item;
struct scrn_buf *screen_data;
```

This function causes the data in the collection area as pointed to by the scrn_buf structure to be written in the proper place on the screen. The caller specifies the screen number and the data item number (relative to one) and provides a pointer to the scrn_buf structure that is in effect for the screen. It is the caller's responsibility to know that the correct template is displayed on the screen. The function takes care of the rest. The data values to be displayed are taken from the standard data collection space for the data item. The function is useful for displaying a new data value without going through scrn_proc for the entire screen.

```
char get_item (sc, crt, fld)
struct scrn_buf *sc;
int crt;
int fld;
```

This function is called when the caller wants to retrieve data from a screen for a given field without going through scrn_proc for the entire screen. The data value is entered by the user and stored into the data space pointed to in the scrn_buf structure. The function returns the keystroke that terminated the entry or '\0' to indicate that entry was terminated when the data field was filled by entered characters.

```
VOID reset_screens ()
```

This function is called when the application is done with the screen management functions. It releases the memory that was allocated for screen buffers. If this function isn't used, the memory won't be there later when another program needs it.

Summary

The screen management subsystem makes a significant addition to the tool collection. We can now control program execution, manage data files, and perform complex interactive data entry.

Next we need to develop methods for management and arrangement of data under different situations in response to different requirements.

Chapter 10 introduces "Sort," a subsystem that lets us change the original order of the records of data in our files. Then, in Chapter 11, we discuss the B-tree technique of inverted data indexing.

10

Data
Sorting

This chapter introduces the toolset functions for data sorting. Often a collection of data needs to be rearranged into a sequence other than the one it presently maintains. The data might come from a file, or the data might be a combination of records from several files. The records might be collected for a report or for a query response, or they might just be passed to another program.

The B-tree indexing functions in Chapter 11 provide for one method of sorting. Any data element from a file that is indexed with a B-tree can be used to form an ascending or a descending sort of the file. The file need not be sorted into a second file in the sequence of the data element. That is one of the advantages of B-trees.

There are other occasions when you will want to order data in sequences not represented by an index. Perhaps the ordered data element is not normally used for on-line retrieval, so no index exists. Or, just as often, the sort sequence required consists of the use of several data elements from the records, sometimes involving a mix of ascending and descending sorts among the different data elements.

One way to solve the sorting problem is to use a file sorting program. This choice is usually good. A sort program reads a file and sorts it as specified by a set of parameters. The sorted records are written to another file. This procedure will usually support any sorting requirement. However, one kind of sort is not supported by most file sort programs. That is the "in-line" sort. An in-line sort is one where the application code module passes data records to the sort procedures and then retrieves the records from them in the specified sequence. The COBOL SORT verb works like that. Also, many data base management system (DBMS) languages contain in-line sorts.

There are a number of advantages to an in-line sort. Among them are:

- You can include the sort process as a part of the interactive session without requiring the system to exit the program, sort a file and execute a different program to process the sorted data.
- It is not necessary to build a discrete file to be sorted. As records of data are developed, they can be passed to the in-line sort.
- The sorted data need not be sent to an output file. The records can be passed one at a time directly to the process that needs it.

On the other hand, there are advantages to sort packages. For example, a general sort package is usually written in assembly language and is considerably faster than anything we can write in most high-level languages.

Sorting Data Using the Toolset

Large volumes of records are sorted in groups, and then the groups are merged. This method is necessary when the records do not all fit into memory at once. So, two data sorting techniques are implemented, the internal sort of groups of records and the merging of these groups. This combination of methods is called, simply, "Sort." To use Sort, the calling function must first provide specifications for the sort, including record size and the sort field descriptions. Sort establishes the sort buffer on the basis of how much memory is available. Then Sort is ready to order the records by using the three phases shown in Figure 10-1.

In Phase 1, the calling program passes the records to Sort one at a time. Sort moves the records into its sort buffer and builds an array of pointers to each one. The pointer array is initially in serial ascending sequence. When the buffer is full, Sort sorts the pointers to the records and then writes the records to a work file by using the sorted array of pointers to determine the proper sequence. This set of ordered records is called a "sequence." Phase 1 continues until Sort is told that there are no more records, at which time either some sequences are on the work file, or all of

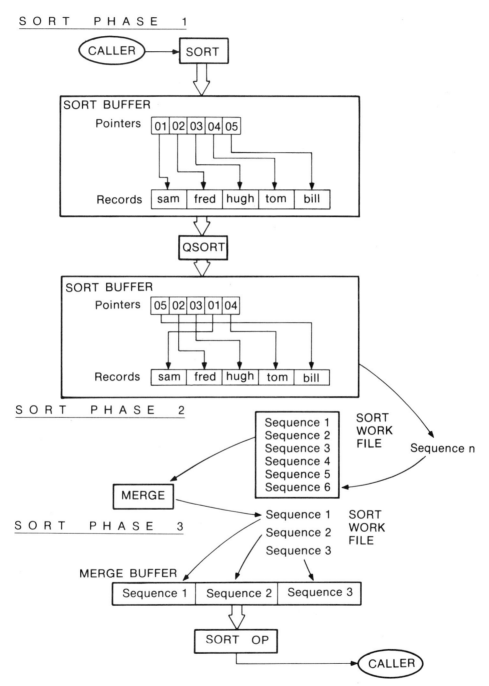

Figure 10-1. The three phases of Sort.

the records to be sorted are still in the sort buffer. In the latter case, the pointers are sorted and Phase 2 is bypassed.

Phase 2 sets up the sorted sequences so that they can be merged into order and passed to the caller. The method used is to divide the merge buffer into several blocks of records, with one block for each work file sequence. If there are more sequences on disk than blocks in the merge buffer, Phase 2 executes a binary merge, where the sequences in the work file are merged together. Each execution of the merge results in one half the number of sequences. This continues until there are fewer sequences on disk than blocks in the merge buffer. Each block in the merge buffer is now filled with records from the sequences, and Sort returns to the calling function.

In Phase 3, the calling function asks Sort to return the records in sequence one at a time. This return of records is actually the return of a pointer to the next sequential record. The record itself remains in the buffer space belonging to Sort. Calling functions must be careful to copy the record into their own space if data in the record must survive successive calls to Sort for more records. If Phase 2 was bypassed, the records in the sort buffer are returned to the caller one at a time, and the sorted pointer array indicates the proper order of records. If Phase 2 was executed, Sort selects the lowest sequence record from the merge buffer and returns it to the caller. When a block in the merge buffer becomes empty, Sort replenishes it with records from the work file as long as some records remain in that particular sequence. When there are no more records to be returned, Sort returns a null pointer.

You can see in Figure 10-1 that Sort does not sort the data records in the sort buffer. As the records are placed into the buffer, an array of pointers to the records is built. The sort algorithm rearranges the pointers rather than the records. This technique proves to be more efficient because the records could be quite long, and the sort would need to exchange a lot of them to achieve the desired sequence. It is quicker to exchange pointers.

Sort Examples

To use the Sort functions for an in-line sort, a program is written that follows the procedure shown in Figure 10-2. It is not necessary to use any of the other toolset functions in order to use Sort. The example program "sortexmp.c" in Listing 10-1 is an illustration of this.

```
/* -------------------------- sortexmp.c -------------------------- */

#include <stdio.h>
#include "toolset.h"
#if COMPILER != CWARE
#if COMPILER != MWC
#include <fcntl.h>
#endif
#endif
#include "sort.h"
#include "member.h"
#include "filhdr.h"

int m_ctr = 0;
VOID roster(), ent_wait();

main()
{
    struct fil_hdr fh;
    long rctr = 0;
    struct mbr_rcd m;                /* member.dat record */
    int *mp, fd;
    static struct s_prm s = {        /* sort parameters */
        sizeof(struct mbr_rcd), /* record size */
        0,                           /* work file drive */
        {7,10,'A'}                   /* field 1, position, length, sequence */
    };

    if (init_sort(&s) == OK)    {
        printf("\n\nSorting...\n");
        fd = open("members.dat", O_RDONLY);
        read(fd, &fh, sizeof(struct fil_hdr));
        mp = (int *) &m;
        while (read(fd, &m, sizeof m) == sizeof m)
            if (fh.nxt_rcd ) ++rctr && *mp != -1)
                sort(mp);
        sort((char *) NULL);
        ent_wait();
        while ((mp = (int *) sort_op()) != NULL)
            roster(mp);
        printf("\n\n%d Members", m_ctr);
        close(fd);
        ent_wait();
        clr_scrn();
        sort_stats();
        ent_wait();
    }
    else
        printf("\n\nInsufficient memory to sort!");
    exit(0);
}
```

Listing 10-1.

Listing 10-1 (continued)

```
/* ----------------------- write the membership roster -------------- */
#define SCLINES 18                       /* # lines on the screen */
VOID roster(mp)
struct mbr_rcd *mp;
{
    static int line_ctr = SCLINES + 1, page_ctr = 0;

    if (line_ctr ) SCLINES) {
        line_ctr = 0;
        if (page_ctr)
            ent_wait();
        clr_scrn();
        printf("\f\rMembership Roster                    Page %d",++page_ctr);
        printf("\nMember Name                    Number");
        printf("\n---------------------------- -----");
    }
    line_ctr++;
    printf("\n%-30s %5s", mp->mbr_nm, mp->mbr_no);
    m_ctr++;
}


VOID ent_wait()
{
    printf("\n\nPress ENTER to continue...\n");
    while (get_byte() != '\r')
        ;
}
```

The processing sequence is as follows. First, a structure of type s_prm, as defined in sort.h, is built. Then, arrangements are made to get the data to be sorted. In the simplest case, this step involves opening a file. Then the sort functions are initialized. Each input record is developed (usually by reading a record from a file) and passed to the sort. When there are no more records to be sorted, a NULL value is passed to the sort. Next, a function is called to retrieve the sorted records one at a time from the sort so that they can be processed, perhaps into a report as in example.c. When the sort returns a NULL value, there are no more sorted records, and the process is over. The open files are closed, and, optionally, the sort statistics are displayed.

The program "sortxmp.c" (Listing 10-1) is an example of the use of the in-line sort. It reads the file "members.dat" (Listing 10-2), which is created by the program "example.c" (from Chapter 12), sorts the records into member-name sequence, and writes a simple report to the printer. It is connected to the program "menuexmp.c" (Chapter 8), but can be run by itself. The program does not use the file management functions to read the file. Those functions are best used for random access because of performance considerations. Therefore, the program has to be aware of the structure of a file manager file, since members.dat is created by the file manager (in the program example.c). Notice that the program bypasses the file header record. The format of the header is found in the file "filhdr.h." Then, as records are read, the program bypasses any records with the integer value −1 in the first two bytes of the record. These records represent ones that have been deleted. Finally, the program uses the value in the variable nxt_rcd from the file header to determine when it has arrived at the last record. This program provides a good example of how to code for serial access to a file manager file.

```
/* --------------------- member.h --------------------------- */

struct mbr_rcd {          /* member.dat record */
    char mbr_no [6];
    char mbr_nm [31];
    char addr1  [31];
    char addr2  [31];
    char city   [31];
    char state  [3];
    char zip    [6];
    char phone  [11];
    char dues   [7];
    char mbr_ty [2];
    char exp_dt [7];
};
```

Listing 10-2.

The program "sorttest.c" (Listing 10-3) is a variation on "sortexmp.c." It takes a different approach to the sort problem. In "sortexmp.c," the records are themselves sorted. The sort_op function returns pointers to complete records. In "sorttest.c," the input records are read, and pseudorecords are built to be sorted. These records contain only the sort key element and the record address. Then, as sort_op returns the sorted pseudorecords in sorted sequence, the program uses the record address to read the complete record from the original file. Which of these approaches are used depends upon an understanding of the file contents. If the records from the file all fit into the sort buffer, then the first technique yields the faster sort time. If, however, there are far more records than can be held in one buffer causing multiple sequences to be sorted and then merged, then the latter technique is preferred.

```
/* ------------------------- sorttest.c ------------------------- */

#include <stdio.h>
#include "toolset.h"
#if COMPILER != CWARE
#if COMPILER != MWC
#include <fcntl.h>
#endif
#endif
#include "sort.h"
#include "member.h"
#include "filhdr.h"
```

Listing 10-3.

Listing 10-3 (continued)

```
int m_ctr = 0;
VOID roster(), ent_wait();

main(argc, argv)
int argc;
char *argv[];
{
    struct fil_hdr fh;
    long rctr = 0;
    struct mbr_rcd m;        /* member.dat record */
    int *mp, fd;
    struct srr {             /* sorted record */
        char snm [10];       /* 10 chars of name */
        ADDR sad;            /* file record address */
        } sr;
    struct srr *srp;
    static struct s_prm s = {      /* sort parameters */
        sizeof(struct srr),        /* sort record length */
        0,                         /* work file drive */
        {1, sizeof sr.snm, 'A'}    /* field 1: position, length, sequence */
    };

    if (init_sort(&s) != OK)    {
        printf("\n\nInsufficient memory to sort!");
        exit();
    }
    printf("\nSorting...");
    fd = open("members.dat", O_RDONLY);
    read(fd, &fh, sizeof(struct fil_hdr));
    mp = (int *) &m;
    while (read(fd, &m, sizeof m) == sizeof m)
        if (fh.nxt_rcd ) ++rctr && *mp != -1)    {
            movmem(m.mbr_nm, sr.snm, sizeof sr.snm);
            sr.sad = rctr;
            sort(&sr);
        }
    sort((char *) NULL);
    while ((srp = (struct srr *) sort_op()) != NULL){
        lseek(fd, (long) (srp->sad - 1) * sizeof m + sizeof fh, 0);
        read(fd, &m, sizeof m);
        roster(&m);
    }
    printf( "\n\n%d Members", m_ctr);

        sort_stats();
        close(fd);
    }
```

Stand-alone Sort

The "stand-alone sort" was mentioned earlier. It is used to sort a file into a new sequence. It reads a named file, sorts it, and writes a new file in the new sequence. The files are identical except for their names and their sequences.

The program "sasort.c" (Listing 10-4) is a stand-alone sort. It uses the Sort functions just described and a file of sort parameters to tell it what file to sort, what file to create, and the sequence for sorting. For its use, a file of parameters is prepared to specify the file format and the sort sequence. To run it, enter:

        sasort filename

where filename is the name of the parameter file. When the program terminates, a new file in the sorted sequence has been built.

```
/* ----------------------- sasort.c ----------------------- */

#include (stdio.h)
#include "toolset.h"
#if COMPILER != CWARE
#if COMPILER != MWC
#include (fcntl.h)
#endif
#endif
#include "sort.h"
#include "sortparm.h"
#include "filhdr.h"
#define BLKPAD 0x1a1a    /* block padding character in some systems (CTRL-Z) */

main(argc, argv)
int argc;
char *argv [];
{
    char c;
    int i, fd, fdin, fdout;
    struct sort_data sd;
    struct s_prm sp;
    struct fil_hdr fh;
    int *p;
    char *malloc();

    if (argc != 2 || (fd = open(argv [1], O_RDONLY)) == ERROR){
        printf("\nInvalid command line");
        exit();
    }
    read(fd, &sd, sizeof(sd));
    close(fd);
    setmem(&sp, sizeof(sp), '\0');
```

Listing 10-4.

Listing 10-4 (continued)

```
sp.rc_len = atoi(sd.rcdlen);
sp.sort_drive = *sd.wrkdrv == ' ' ? 0 : toupper(*sd.wrkdrv) - 'A' + 1;
for (i = 0; i < NOFLDS; i++)
    if (*sd.fs [i].pos != ' ')          {
        sp.s_fld [i].f_pos = atoi(sd.fs [i].pos);
        sp.s_fld [i].f_len = atoi(sd.fs [i].len);
        sp.s_fld [i].az    = *sd.fs [i].saz;
    }
if ((fdin = open(sd.infile, O_RDONLY)) == ERROR){
    printf("\nInput file not found");
    exit();
}
if ((c = toupper(*sd.wsfilein)) == 'Y')
    read(fdin, &fh, sizeof(struct fil_hdr));
if ((p = (int *) malloc(sp.rc_len)) == 0 || init_sort(&sp) == ERROR){
    printf("\nInsufficient memory to sort");
    exit();
}
while (read(fdin, p, sp.rc_len) == sp.rc_len){
    if (*p == BLKPAD)
        break;
    if (*p != -1 || c != 'Y')
        sort(p);

        else
            --fh.nxt_rcd;
    }
    sort((char *) NULL);
    close(fdin);
    fd = creat(sd.otfile, CMODE);
    close(fd);
    fdout = open(sd.otfile, O_WRONLY);
    if (toupper(*sd.wsfileout) == 'Y')  {
        fh.fst_rcd = 0;
        write(fdout, &fh, sizeof(struct fil_hdr));
    }
    while ((p = (int *) sort_op()) != NULL)
        write(fdout, p, sp.rc_len);
    close(fdout);
    sort_stats();
    free(p);
}
```

The program "sortparm.c" (Listing 10-5) is to help you build the parameters. It uses the screen management functions for parameter data entry and the file "sortparm.crt" (the contents of sortparm.crt are shown in Figure 10-3) to describe the parameter screen template. Both "sasort.c" and "sortparm.c" use "sortparm.h" (Listing 10-6) to describe the format of the sort parameter file.

```c
/* ------------------------- sortparm.c ------------------------- */

#include <stdio.h>
#include "toolset.h"
#if COMPILER != CWARE
#if COMPILER != MWC
#include <fcntl.h>
#endif
#endif
#include "sort.h"
#include "screen.h"
#include "keys.h"
#include "sortparm.h"

main(argc, argv)
int argc;
char *argv [];
{
    char c;
    static char dname [] = "            ";
    int i, fd;
    static struct sort_data sd;
    int ynedit(), azedit();
    static struct scrn_buf sr [] = {
        {'A', TRUE,  dname,         0,      0, TRUE, FALSE, 0},
        {'A', FALSE, sd.infile,     0,      0, TRUE, FALSE, 0},
        {'A', FALSE, sd.wsfilein,   ynedit, 0, TRUE, FALSE, 0},
        {'A', FALSE, sd.otfile,     0,      0, TRUE, FALSE, 0},
        {'A', FALSE, sd.wsfileout,  ynedit, 0, TRUE, FALSE, 0},
        {'Z', FALSE, sd.rcdlen,     0,      0, TRUE, FALSE, 0},
        {'A', FALSE, sd.wrkdrv,     0,      0, TRUE, FALSE, 0},
        {'Z', FALSE, sd.fs[0].pos,  0,      0, TRUE, FALSE, 0},
        {'Z', FALSE, sd.fs[0].len,  0,      0, TRUE, FALSE, 0},
        {'A', FALSE, sd.fs[0].saz,  azedit, 0, TRUE, FALSE, 0},
        {'Z', FALSE, sd.fs[1].pos,  0,      0, TRUE, FALSE, 0},
        {'Z', FALSE, sd.fs[1].len,  0,      0, TRUE, FALSE, 0},
        {'A', FALSE, sd.fs[1].saz,  azedit, 0, TRUE, FALSE, 0},
        {'Z', FALSE, sd.fs[2].pos,  0,      0, TRUE, FALSE, 0},
        {'Z', FALSE, sd.fs[2].len,  0,      0, TRUE, FALSE, 0},
        {'A', FALSE, sd.fs[2].saz,  azedit, 0, TRUE, FALSE, 0},
        {'Z', FALSE, sd.fs[3].pos,  0,      0, TRUE, FALSE, 0},
```

Listing 10-5.

Listing 10-5 (continued)

```
        {'Z', FALSE, sd.fs[3].len, 0,        0, TRUE, FALSE, 0},
        {'A', FALSE, sd.fs[3].saz, azedit, 0, TRUE, FALSE, 0},
        {'Z', FALSE, sd.fs[4].pos, 0,        0, TRUE, FALSE, 0},
        {'Z', FALSE, sd.fs[4].len, 0,        0, TRUE, FALSE, 0},
        {'A', FALSE, sd.fs[4].saz, azedit, 0, TRUE, FALSE, 0}
    };

    if (argc == 2)    {
        setmem(&sd, sizeof(sd), ' ');
        if ((fd = open(argv[1], O_RDWR)) == -1)
            fd = creat(argv[1], CMODE);
        read(fd, &sd, sizeof(sd));
        read_screens("sortparm.crt");
        strcpy(dname, argv[1]);
        c = scrn_proc(1, sr, FALSE);

        clr_scrn();
        if (c != ESC)    {
            lseek(fd, 0L, 0);
            write(fd,  &sd, sizeof(sd));
            printf("\n\nWriting sort parameter file %s",argv[1]);
        }
        reset_screens();
        close(fd);
    }
    else
        printf("\nInvalid command line");
}

int ynedit(p, c)
char *p, c;
{
    char ch;

    ch = toupper(*p);
    if (ch == 'Y' || ch == 'N' || ch == ' ')
        return OK;
    err_msg("Y or N only");
    return ERROR;
}



int azedit(p, c)
char *p, c;
{
```

Listing 10-5 (continued)

```
char ch;

ch = toupper(*p);
if (ch == 'A' || ch == 'Z' || ch == ' ')
    return OK;
err_msg("A or Z only");
return ERROR;
}
```

```
*


              Sort Definition _____


                          Toolset FM File
        Files                 (Y/N)
        ..........          ........................
        Input  _____       [__]

        Output_____        [__]


  Record Length: _____  Work File Drive: [__]

                 Byte                 A = Ascending,
        Field    Position   Length    Z = Descending

          1.     _____    _____       [__]
          2.     _____    _____       [__]
          3.     _____    _____       [__]
          4.     _____    _____       [__]
          5.     _____    _____       [__]
```

Figure 10-3. The contents of sortparm.crt.

```
/* -------------------- sortparm.h -------------------------- */

struct sort_data  {
    char infile     [15];        /* input file name*/
    char wsfilein   [2];         /* 'y' = i/p file = Toolset*/
    char otfile     [15];        /* output file name*/
    char wsfileout  [2];         /* 'y' = o/p file = Toolset*/
    char rcdlen     [5];         /* records length*/
    char wrkdrv     [2];         /* work file drive #*/
    struct {
```

Listing 10-6.

Listing 10-6 (continued)

```
        char pos [5];          /* sort field position*/
        char len [4];          /* sort field length*/
        char saz [2];          /* a = ascending, z = descending*/
    }   fs [NOFLDS];           /* one per sort field*/
};
```

To run "sortparm.c," enter the following command line:

```
sortparm filename
```

where filename is the name of the sort parameter file you wish to either build or modify. The screen template shown as "sortparm. crt" appears on the screen. If you called for an existing parameter file, the contents of it are displayed on the screen. You can enter the names of the file to be sorted and the new file with the new sequence. You must fill in the blocks that specify, for both files, if the file is in the file manager format; that is, if the file being sorted was created by the file management functions, and if the new file is to be compatible with the file management functions. Files in this format contain a header record that must be bypassed on input and re-created on output. These files also contain a deleted record mark identifying records that have been deleted. Deleted records are bypassed on input and not re-created on output.

The Sort Functions

These are the functions called to have Sort sort records of data. These functions are reusable; that is, once one sort is completed, the same program can use the functions to sort other data. It is important that the sort be carried to completion because there is a large block of memory allocated for the sort buffer which is not returned to the system until all the sorting is done.

```
int init_sort (prms)
struct s_prm *prms;
```

This function is called before any sorting is begun to initialize the sort parameters. The calling program should have the file "sort.h" from Appendix A included in its source. This provides the structure s_prm for the sort parameters.

Prior to calling the init_sort function, set up a structure of type s_prm. The call to `init_sort` includes a pointer to your structure. This pointer is made global so if you are using tricky overlays, beware. Most of the Sort functions use this pointer, so the memory area occupied by the structure must be available throughout the sort.

Place the record length into `rcd_len`. Indicate the disk drive you want used for the sort work file in sort_drive. Use 0 for the current logged-on drive, 1 for drive A, 2 for drive B, and so on. These are CP/M and MS-DOS conventions. Other operating systems may need a different drive specifier, and the code that deals with it may need to be modified. The C language does not address this issue.

The expression NOFLDS is defined in sort.h. It specifies the maximum number of sort fields that can be used in a sort. Initialize with the following values in the structure for each sort field:

- `f_pos` is the field's position in the record relative to one.
- `f_len` is the field's length in characters.
- `az` is a flag indicating the sequence of the sort. 'A' means ascending, 'Z' means descending.

The fields are sorted in the order in which they occur in the structure. The first field in the array is the major sort field, and the last field is the minor sort field.

Init_sort returns ERROR if insufficient memory is available for the specified sort; otherwise, it returns OK. Two global definitions in the file sort.c control how much memory is allocated. The first, MOSTMEM, specifies the amount of memory that `init_sort` tries to get as a buffer. If that much is not available, then subsequent attempts are made by reducing the requested amount by 1024 bytes. This continues until a block of memory is allocated or until the requested amount gets below the value in the global LEASTMEM. That global specifies the least amount of memory that would be acceptable. Adjust these values to reflect the machine's memory size and the compiler's memory model. As published, they work with Aztec C86 for the IBM PC using the small (128K) memory model.

```
sort (s_rcd)
char *s_rcd;
```

This function is called to give records to Sort. When there is a record to be sorted, call this function, passing it a pointer to the record. When there are no more records, pass a pointer with the value NULL.

```
char *sort_op ()
```

This function is called to get sorted records back from Sort. Make calls to **sort_op** to get each successive record. A pointer to the next record is returned. The record is located out somewhere in the sort buffer, so be careful with it. When there are no more records to be returned, **sort_op** returns a NULL pointer. Be sure and call **sort_op** until the NULL is returned. Otherwise, the large allocated sort buffer is not returned to the system, and subsequent requests for memory will fail.

```
sort_stats ()
```

This function can be called after the sorting is complete to cause a display of sort characteristics. The display consists of a series of lines that start wherever the cursor is located. They are generally of interest only to the programmer and not to the user, although users often like to see these kinds of things. Use them while testing and then remove them from the operational program. The information displayed includes:

- the length of the records being sorted
- the total number of records sorted
- the number of sequences—the number of times the sort buffer was filled
- the size of the sort buffer
- the number of records a sort buffer held

```
int comp (a, b)
char *a, *b;
```

This function compares records for sorting and merging. It is not called by the application software, but it may be customized.

Because it is table-driven by the entries in your sort parameters, it can be very slow. It expects **a** and **b** to point to the two records to compare and returns an integer that is less than 0 if the record pointed to by **a** compares less than the the one pointed to by **b**, greater than 0 if the reverse is true, and equal to 0 if the two records compare equally. If the compare includes fields that are to be sorted in descending sequence, the result is adjusted. Incidentally, the `comp` function, as coded, sorts by machine collating sequence. You may wish to have it sort upper- and lowercase alphabetic characters together or to properly deal with signed integers or floating point numbers. To do so, you must modify it.

Summary

Data file sorting has been required ever since information found its way onto cards. In this chapter we implemented data sorting both as an in-line sort in our own programs, and as a stand-alone file sorting program. There is another data ordering requirement that is inseparable from the on-line, interactive system. To be interactive, you must be able to get at a desired record in a hurry. One way to do so is to build an index similar to the index in a book. Using the indexed value, you look up the location of the data in the index, and then you go directly to the data. In data systems, such indices are referred to as "inverted indices." That is the subject of Chapter 11, the use of B-trees as an inverted indexing technique.

B-Tree
Index
Management

11

You can retrieve a record of data a number of ways once it has been stored away. The most familiar technique is to write data in the order in which it occurs and to read the records in the same sequence. Processes requiring the data records in other sequences use a file sorting utility program. In Chapter 10 we learned to take a file of data originally arranged in one sequence and sort it into another so that a query or report could be prepared. This method is necessary because the records are stored in a sequence other than the one needed for the current purpose.

File sorting works well in the off-line, batch environment; but, in the on-line, interactive environment, serial data retrieval is usually too slow to be acceptable, thus, on-line sorting is not used very often because demands for the data usually occur at random intervals requiring random retrievals of records. Often those retrievals require instant access to data on the basis of various selection criteria. The software functions in this chapter address that problem.

These functions allow you to maintain multiple inverted indexes for a data file. An index is a technique for finding a record in a file on the basis of the value of a data element. Besides the file of data, a supporting file contains the index. The index is a list of all of the values for the data element, each one connected to a pointer to the record containing the value. If a file is indexed on several data elements (keys), then a record in that file can be located by using any of the indexed key values. Figure 11-1 shows the concept of an inverted index. The index in this example has abbreviations of states that point to data file records containing the abbreviations and the names of the states. An index is effective when retrieval of a given value from the index is faster than retrieval of the same value from the data file. The B-tree is a method of inverted indexing that delivers that kind of performance.

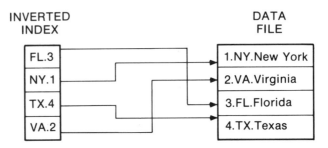

Figure 11-1. An inverted index.

What is a B-tree?

A B-tree is a hierarchical structure of records called "nodes." The nodes contain indexed key data element values and pointers. The structure is that of an upside down tree with the root node at the top and the leaf nodes at the bottom. Nodes at the intermediate level (neither the root nor a leaf) are simply called nodes. Figure 11-2 is an illustration of a B-tree. The pointers in the nodes support the structure. In the leaf nodes, the pointers point to data records. In the nonleaf nodes, the pointers point to lower nodes (toward the leaves) in the tree. If a B-tree has only one node, it is the root and the only leaf.

Mixed metaphors are common in this discipline. The vertical relationships between nodes are called parent–child, and horizontal relationships are sibling or cousin relationships, all in a tree with a root and leaves. Perhaps it is a family tree.

Figure 11-2 is an example of a simple B-tree where the indexed keys are, again, the abbreviations of some of the (American) states. In the figure, the pointers are represented by dots with arrows showing where they point. The keys in the nodes are actually maintained in their proper sequence. The bottom of the tree consists of its leaves. The pointers in the leaves are pointing to the file records that contain the values that are indexed. These file records are not part of the B-tree; they are not in the B-tree file, and they are not a part of the B-tree architecture. In the figure, the file records represent the files of data that are stored in random sequence and are indexed by the B-tree. This figure is an explosion of the construct shown in Figure 11-1.

A node contains a fixed maximum number of keys based upon the key length. This constant, the number of keys in a node, is referred to as m, and a tree with m − 1 keys and m pointers in the node is called an "m − way tree." The insertion and deletion logic of B-trees provides for dynamic balancing of the tree, meaning that the path from the root to any leaf always involves the same number of accesses. All nodes except the root node contain at least (m − 1)/2 keys, and no more than m − 1 keys. The root node can contain from 1 to m − 1 keys. In Figure 11-2, m is equal to 4. The figure is not typical because all of the nodes are full. This was done to illustrate the key insertion discussion later.

Searching a B-tree

The search of a B-tree consists of proceeding from the root downward to the leaves, comparing the key values in the nodes to a specified key argument. Here is the procedure for searching a B-tree.

1. Begin with the root node.
2. Search the node from left to right for the first key equal to or greater than the search argument. If an equal is found, the search is over, and the argument is in the B-tree.
3. If the search ends on a key value greater than the argument, and the node being searched is a leaf, the search is over and the argument is not in the B-tree.
4. If the search ends on a key value greater than the argument, and the node is not a leaf, use the pointer to the left of the key value which terminated the search to retrieve the next lower node. Return to step 2.

Using the B-tree in Figure 11-2 and the search procedure, try to find an entry for the state of Florida on the basis of the key value FL. Try to find one for New Jersey.

Once a key has been found, the file address must also be found. If the key is in a leaf, then the pointer to the immediate right of the key is the file pointer (points to the record in the file being indexed that contains this key). For example, in Figure 11-2 the

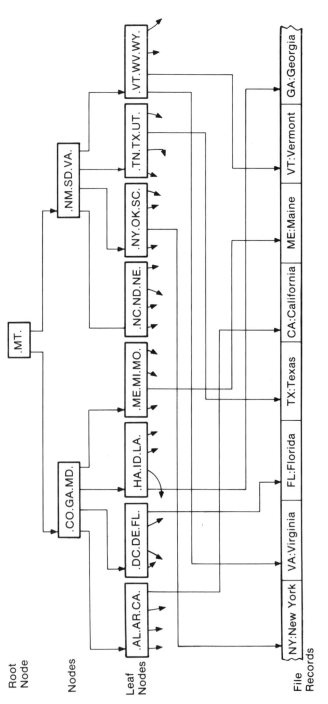

Figure 11-2. A B-tree.

pointer to the right of the value NY in the third leaf node from the right end points to the file record for the state of New York.

If the matching key is not in a leaf, then the pointer points to a lower node rather than a file record, and the leaf node must be located to find the file address. Notice that in Figure 11-2, the file address for Georgia is the left-most pointer of the leaf node pointed to by the GA key value. To navigate down to a leaf from a given key value in a nonleaf node, follow this procedure:

1. Use the pointer to the right of the key to retrieve the next lower node.
2. If that node is not a leaf, use the left-most pointer from that node to retrieve the next lower node. Repeat this step.
3. When the most recent node retrieved is a leaf, use the left-most pointer as the file address.

Which of the pointers in Figure 11-2 is for the state of Montana (MT)?

Key Insertion

When a B-tree is initially built and, subsequently, when it is updated, keys are inserted into the tree. The insertion algorithms must be able to insert keys regardless of the original sequence of the keys, and they must be able to do so while still maintaining the balance of the tree.

The first step of key insertion involves locating the proper place in the tree for the new key. This step uses the search procedure just shown. If the key value does not already exist in the tree, the search procedure ends at the point in a leaf where insertion is to occur. From there, the insertion procedures are as follows:

1. Insert the key value into the leaf along with the file pointer. This insertion must maintain the collating sequence of the keys in the leaf node. If the node contains fewer than m keys, the insertion is complete.
2. If the node now contains m keys, split the node into two sibling nodes, distribute the keys between the two, and hold out the middle key to be inserted into the parent node. The parent of the two nodes is the same as the parent of the original node before splitting. If there was, in fact, a parent, establish the withheld key as one to be inserted into the parent and return to step 1.

3. If the node that was just split had no parent, then the split node is the root node (the only orphan in the family). Since the root node was just split and there is a withheld key without a node to go home to, a new root node must be created, and the lone key is inserted into it. The new root node becomes the parent of the two nodes just split.

Sometimes the splitting of a node can be avoided. If there is a sibling node on one side of the node being processed, and if the contents of the two can be redistributed so that both of them have less than **m** nodes, then a split is not necessary.

The term "sibling" is used in a loose context. Look at the two nodes that begin with values ME and NC in Figure 11-2. For the purpose of this discussion, they are siblings. But, they are actually cousins. They have different parents and their parents are themselves siblings. This becomes important when the keys are redistributed among adjacent nodes. Key deletion can cause adjacent nodes to be combined or their keys to be redistributed for a more even balance of key population among nodes. This only occurs between true siblings.

Let's use the B-tree in Figure 11-2 to illustrate key insertion. Suppose that we want to insert a record for the state of New Jersey with the key value of NJ into the B-tree. After Step 1, the third leaf node from the right looks like this:

.NC.ND.NE.NJ.

Since the node now contains **m** keys, one more than it should, and since both sibling nodes are full, it is necessary to split the node, holding out the middle key for insertion into the parent. The split results in two nodes like this:

.NC.ND.   .NJ.

The key value, NE, is held out and must now be inserted into the parent of the split nodes, which is the right-most of the two nodes on the second level. This insertion has this result:

.NE.NM.SD.VA.

Now, this node is too full, so it is split as follows:

```
.NE.NM.        .VA.
```

The withheld key value, SD, is now inserted into the parent of these two nodes, which happens to be the root node and looks like this after the insertion:

```
.MT.SD.
```

The root node is not at capacity, so it does not need to be split. If it did, the withheld key would go by itself into a new node that would become the new root node.

After all of that inserting and splitting, the tree looks a bit different. Here is a fragment of it, representing the part of the tree that changed.

Root
Node

```
.MT.SD.
```

```
.NE.NM.                                    .VA.
```

Leaf
Nodes

```
.NC.ND.    .NJ.    .NY.OK.SC.    .TN.TX.UT.    .VT.WV.WY.
```

Key Deletion

To delete a key, its location is found in the B-tree with the search procedure just defined. To maintain tree balance, keys are initially deleted from leaf nodes. If the key to be deleted is in a nonleaf node, that key is replaced with the first key in the lower leaf node that is traced from the key to be deleted. Then the first key is deleted from the leaf.

For example, deletion of the key with the value GA from the B-tree in Figure 11-2 begins with the movement of key HA from the leaf node up and over the top of key GA.

Next the pointer to the Georgia file record and the key value HA from the leaf node are deleted. The remaining three pointers and two keys are shifted to the left so that the node looks like this:

.ID.LA.

The first pointer points to Hawaii, the second points to Idaho, and the third points to Louisiana.

If the deletion of a key causes that node to become under-populated (that is, it has less than (m − 1)/2 nodes), then the keys of this node and one of its siblings are redistributed. If possible, the contents of two nodes are combined. This combination requires the deletion of a key in the parent node. The key in the parent that points between the two child nodes is moved down into the new combined node and must be deleted from the parent. When that happens, the delete process proceeds upward toward the root. Only then are keys deleted from nonleaf nodes.

Tree Balance

The "B" in B-tree stands for "balanced." A balanced tree is one where the path from the root to any leaf involves as many accesses as to any other leaf. In Figure 11-2, this path would involve three accesses. When a tree "grows" a level, the growth always occurs when the root node splits into two and grows a new root with a single key. When that happens, the number of accesses to any leaf increases by one, and the tree remains in balance. When enough keys are deleted from a node, its contents are combined with the keys from one of its sibling nodes. This means that one key is deleted from the parent of the two. If the last key is deleted from the root node as the result of this process, then its two former child nodes have been combined into one, and the combined node becomes the new root. This process reduces the number of levels in the tree by one, and balance is maintained. Other tree structures, such as the binary tree, do not have this balanced property. The balanced tree is an effective structure because of the speed and efficiency with which search, insertion, and deletion can be performed.

What's in a Node?

A node, as we have seen, contains keys and pointers. Figure 11-3 shows the other things that a node contains. These exist for the convenience of the algorithms. First is a flag that indicates whether the node is a leaf or not. Several of the algorithms need to know at once if they are working with a leaf or a nonleaf. Next is the node number of the parent of this node. If this is the root node, then this value is null. Next are the node numbers of the left and right siblings of the node. If either does not exist, then the value is null. The left-most node of any level of the tree has no left sibling, and the right-most node has no right sibling. Last is the number of keys that this node contains, followed by the pointers and keys. There is always one more pointer than the number of keys.

Leaf Flag	Parent Node	Left Sibling Node	Right Sibling Node	Number of Keys This Node	Pointer	Key	Pointer	Key	...etc.

Figure 11-3. The contents of a node.

In the B-tree functions as coded, a node is 512 bytes long. The current implementation is on the IBM PC, so we know that integers are 2 bytes, long integers are 4 bytes, and there are no variable boundary alignments to concern us. The node/leaf flag and the key counter are integers. Each pointer to another node is a long integer, so it occupies four bytes. (The software uses the sizeof operator to compute offsets in case your compiler uses a different integer or long integer length.) So, the data values up to the pointers and keys require sixteen bytes. There are m keys and $m + 1$ pointers. Since the pointers are four bytes each, the formula for computing m for a given key of length b bytes is:

$$m = \big((512 - (\text{sizeof(int)}*2) - \text{sizeof(long)}*4)\big)/(b + \text{sizeof(long)})$$

Remember that this assumes no alignment padding. If your compiler enforces alignment rules, it will be necessary for you to round up the value of b to the next even multiple of 2 or 4 bytes. Each key in a B-tree node has either an integer or long data type on both sides of it. Which one depends on how you have the data type ADDR defined in the file "toolset.h."

Later, we discuss changing the node length and the variable type of file/node addresses to improve the value of m. A larger m gives dramatic performance improvements, but requires more system memory.

How the Pointers Work

The first pointer in the node points to the node in the next level down that contains keys less than the first key in this node and greater than the last key in the previous adjacent node. Each key in the node is followed by a pointer to the node in the next lower level that contains keys greater than this key and less than the next adjacent key.

The pointers in the leaf point to the file records rather than to lower nodes (which do not exist). The first pointer in each leaf points to the file record of the key in the parent record that points to this node. That key might be more than one level away. Once again, look at Figure 11-2 to get a clear picture of how this works. The left-most pointer in the left-most leaf of the tree points nowhere. This null pointer is because there is no value less than the first key in that leaf. Not all B-tree implementations work exactly this way. Some have no leaves at all, thus allowing the file records to be the leaves. That approach eliminates the bottom level of the tree, which saves a lot of space. However, it requires a tight coupling between the file structure and the tree structure and was avoided for that reason in the toolset software.

By using a long integer for a file pointer, the software supports files with $2**32$ records. This should be enough for any application that uses microcomputers. If your data base is bigger than that, or even anywhere close to that size, I'd suggest you look somewhere other than the IBM PC for your computing support. Many applications can use the unsigned integer as a file pointer, addressing up to 65,535 records, and allowing more keys per node, thus improving the efficiency of the tree.

The Efficiency of the B-Tree

Suppose that in a B-tree the keys are 15 bytes long. Using the formula just shown, you get m equal to 25. This means that each node can hold at most m — 1 or 24 keys. If the tree is densely populated (which will happen if it is initially loaded in key sequence), each node holds 24 keys. But, let's say that over a period of time, through the use of inserts and deletes, the tree now averages 20 keys per node. If the data base contains 8000 records, the tree has three levels. That means that a data record is located and is in memory in no more than four accesses, including the one to read the data. If the root node is kept in memory, that is reduced to three accesses. Consider that! Any desired record out of 8000 can be located and read with only three disk accesses. And all that the B-tree software needs to find it is the key value. The B-tree search software can then find the record and return the file address of the record.

Remember that the B-tree itself requires disk space. Each key in the index has one copy of the key value plus a pointer. There is some additional overhead for the items at the beginning of each node. The formula for computing the disk space in bytes required for an index is as follows:

number of keys / average keys per node * node length

MS-DOS allocates clusters of sectors to files; a file occupies no less than the size of a single cluster and always occupies space equal to an even multiple of the cluster size. So, when computing index size, increase the number to the next highest multiple of the cluster size. Most hard disk implementations have 2048-byte clusters.

The 8000 records with 15-byte keys and a distribution of 20 keys to the node require 204,800 bytes of disk space just for the index. That is 1% of the space on the IBM AT's hard disk. If the index is rebuilt so that every node contains the maximum number of keys (24), then the index requires 170,496 bytes of disk storage. To achieve even further reduction of the index overhead, rebuild the system changing the pointers to unsigned integers instead of long integers. This is possible because only 8000 records need to be addressed. The decrease in pointer size raises the value of m to 29, meaning that 4 more keys fit in a node than before. With densely packed nodes (28 keys per node), 145,920 bytes of disk is used for the index.

A B-Tree Example

Listing 11-1 is a small program that uses the insert, search, and delete functions and special functions for sequential retrieval of keys. It implements the B-tree in Figure 11-2.

The program builds a B-tree with the state abbreviations. Instead of a file, an array of state names is kept in memory. This presentation keeps the program simple for the purpose of the example. The program displays a prompt asking for an abbreviation. If the one typed is in the tree, the program displays the name of the state. Otherwise, a sequential list of all the states in the tree is displayed.

```
/* ------------------------ btreexmp.c ------------------------ */

#include <stdio.h>
#include "toolset.h"
#include "btree.h"

char *code [] = {"NY","VA","FL","TX","CA","ME","VT","GA","NC","SC", 0};
char *name [] = {"New York", "Virginia", "Florida", "Texas", "California",
                "Maine", "Vermont", "Georgia", "North Carolina",
                "South Carolina", 0};
#define show() printf("\n%s:%s",code[(int)ad-1],name[(int)ad-1])

main()
{
    ADDR ad = 0;
    static char abr [] = "    ";
    int tree;
    tree = init_b("states.ndx", 2);
    while (code [(int) ad]) {
        insert_key(tree, code [(int) ad], ad + 1, TRUE);
        ad++;
    }
    while (strcmp(abr, "end"))  {
        printf("\nEnter state abbreviation: ");
        gets(abr);
        if (find_key(tree, abr, &ad))
            show();
        else if (ad = find_first(tree)) {
            show();
            while (ad = get_next(tree))
                show();
        }
    }
    ad = 0;
    while (code [(int) ad]) {
        delete_key(tree, code [(int) ad], ad + 1);
        ad++;
    }
    close_b(tree);
    unlink("states.ndx");
}
```

Listing 11-1

The B-Tree Functions

The C source code included in Appendix A contains the B-tree functions. These are the functions that are called by the applications software modules to perform all of the B-tree processes required by an application, as well as those that are used from within the functions themselves.

This discussion addresses each of the functions called by application programs. Note that some function parameters are defined as being of type ADDR. This is the variable type of a file address and is established by a #define statement in the source file "toolset.h." It must correspond to the desired span of disk record addresses. If your C compiler uses a 16 bit unsigned integer, and no disk file will ever exceed 65,535 logical records, then the #define can equate ADDR to unsigned. In "toolset.h," ADDR is equated to the long type. Using the integer type allows more keys to reside in a node, thus giving a greater m value to a tree. The source code automatically adjusts everything when you change the #define and recompile.

"Toolset.h" should be included in the calling source code. Then type ADDR can be used for the return variables from some functions. This retains the portability of the application code. Later, when the size of the file address is changed, the application code will adjust itself along with the toolset code.

Another variable that can be configured from within "toolset.h" and which will affect the performance of the B-tree functions is the global NODELEN. This is a constant that defines the length in bytes of logical disk and B-tree nodes. The larger the node, the more keys it will hold. The more keys in a node, the fewer levels in a B-tree and the faster the access and update times. All software source code automatically adjusts when the #define NODELEN statement is changed. NODELEN should be a multiple of the disk sector size.

To use these functions, include the following statements in the calling program's source file:

```
#include <toolset.h>
#include <btree.h>
```

```
int init_b (name, len)
int tree;
char *name;
int len;
```

This function initiates B-tree processing for a given tree. The first parameter points to a character array containing the name of the B-tree file.

If the B-tree index file does not exist, the function creates it.

The second parameter, len, is used in building a new index file. It is the byte length of a single key in the index.

If the file exists, this function tests to see if it has been properly closed since its last use. The index must have been processed through the function close_b following its most recent use. If not, something is amiss, and the data in the index cannot be trusted. Chances are there was a power failure the last time this index was used, and the collection of most recently changed buffers was not returned to the disk. Perhaps the application program failed to call close_b when it was finished with the index. In either case, the function terminates processing of the program with a message to that effect. This feature has caused me some grief. Some of my report programs use the B-tree to provide the sort sequence. Sometimes I will abort a report program when I have seen the first several records. If the B-tree doesn't get closed, it will be locked the next time I need it. To get around this, there is a program called unlock.c in Appendix A. It will unlock a specified B-tree file.

If the index is in good order, the function returns a B-tree integer tree number to be included by the caller in subsequent calls to B-tree functions. This integer is referred to as the "tree number" and must be used in all function calls related to the B-tree just opened.

Remember that the close_b function must be called when index processing is done.

```
close_b (tree)
int tree;
```

This function handles the closing of an index after its use by the calling software. All buffers are cleared and the index is marked as closed. The function init_b must be used prior to any further use of this particular index by this or another calling program.

```
int find_key (tree, key, addr)
int tree;
char *key;
ADDR *addr;
```

This function searches for the occurrence of a specified key in the tree. The first parameter, tree, is the tree number that init_b returned to identify this B-tree index. The second is a pointer to a character array containing the key to be searched for. The third is a pointer to a file address. The function puts the file address of the record found into the location pointed to by this parameter. If no matching key is found in the index, the function puts the file address of the next higher key into the location. If the key is greater than any key in the index, the function puts a null value into the location. The function returns TRUE if a match for the key was found in the index and FALSE if no match was found.

```
int insert_key (tree, key, addr, unique)
int tree;
char *key;
ADDR addr;
int unique;
```

This function is used to insert a key into a B-tree index. The first parameter identifies the tree by using the tree number from init_b. The second parameter points to the key to be inserted. The third is the file address to be put into the leaf node of the tree and to be associated with the key. This would be the record number of the record in the file being indexed that contains this key. The third parameter is a TRUE or FALSE to tell the function if this particular tree allows only unique keys—that is, a key value may only appear once in this tree if this parameter is TRUE.

The function returns ERROR if a duplicate key is provided to a tree for which unique keys are specified. Otherwise OK is returned.

```
int delete_key (tree, key, addr)
int tree;
char *key;
ADDR addr;
```

This function is used to delete a key from the B-tree index. The parameters are the tree number, a pointer to the key and the file address of the key to be deleted. So that a key may be deleted, there must be a match on both the key itself and the file address associated with it.

```
ADDR get_next (tree)
int tree;
```

Starting from where the tree is currently positioned, this function locates the next sequential key in a tree on the basis of the most recent access to the tree. If there has been no prior access to the tree, the first key is located. The file address associated with the located key is returned. If the most recent prior access was to the last sequential key in the tree, then NULL is returned. If the tree is empty, NULL is returned.

```
ADDR get_prev (tree)
int tree;
```

Starting from where the tree is currently positioned, this function locates the previous sequential key in a tree on the basis of the most recent access to the tree. If there has been no prior access to the tree, the last key is located. The file address associated with the located key is returned. If the most recent prior access was to the first sequential key in the tree, then NULL is returned. If the tree is empty, NULL is returned.

```
ADDR find_first (tree)
int tree;
```

This function locates the first sequential key in the specified B-tree index and returns its file address. If the tree is empty, the function returns NULL.

```
ADDR find_last (tree)
int tree;
```

This function locates the last sequential key in the specified B-tree index and returns its file address. If the tree is empty, the function returns NULL.

Summary

This chapter concludes the collection of "C Software Development Tools." All of the basic components of an interactive system are here. You will be pleased at the speed and efficiency with which you can deliver an effective, operational software system by using these tools. These are proven concepts, and the functions that you have collected are in use in many of the systems that I have developed for clients.

Chapter 12 presents an example of an on-line program that uses most of the tools from the toolset that we have built in the past several chapters.

12

Toolset Example

Now that we have built a tool collection of C functions for screen management, file management, and B-tree management, we can begin to use them. This chapter presents a program that applies many of the toolset functions. The program is named "example.c" and you can run it by itself or as one of the programs selected from a menu and fetched by "menuexmp.c" from Chapter 8. "Example.c" is shown in Listing 12-1.

```
/* --------------------- example.c ------------------------------ */

#include <stdio.h>
#include "toolset.h"
#if COMPILER != CWARE
#include <ctype.h>
#endif
#include "screen.h"
#include "file.h"
#include "btree.h"
#include "member.h"
#include "terminal.h"
#include "keys.h"

struct mbr_rcd mbr_data;                    /* member.dat record */

char d_city [] = "                          ";/* ditto areas */
char d_st   [] = "  ";
char d_zip  [] = "      ";

int mbr_ty_edit();
int mbr_edit();
char *mbr_help();
```

Listing 12-1.

137

Listing 12-1 (continued)

```
struct scrn_buf mbr [] = {
  { 'Z', FALSE, mbr_data.mbr_no,  mbr_edit,     mbr_help, TRUE,  FALSE, 0     },
  { 'A', FALSE, mbr_data.mbr_nm,  0,            0,        TRUE,  FALSE, 0     },
  { 'A', FALSE, mbr_data.addr1,   0,            0,        TRUE,  FALSE, 0     },
  { 'A', FALSE, mbr_data.addr2,   0,            0,        TRUE,  FALSE, 0     },
  { 'A', FALSE, mbr_data.city,    0,            0,        TRUE,  FALSE, d_city },
  { 'A', FALSE, mbr_data.state,   0,            0,        TRUE,  FALSE, d_st   },
  { 'N', FALSE, mbr_data.zip,     0,            0,        TRUE,  FALSE, d_zip  },
  { 'N', FALSE, mbr_data.phone,   0,            0,        TRUE,  FALSE, 0     },
  { 'C', FALSE, mbr_data.dues,    0,            0,        TRUE,  FALSE, 0     },
  { 'A', FALSE, mbr_data.mbr_ty,  mbr_ty_edit,  0,        TRUE,  FALSE, 0     },
  { 'D', FALSE, mbr_data.exp_dt,  0,            0,        TRUE,  FALSE, 0     }
};

int existing_record = FALSE;          /* flag */
ADDR adr = 0;                         /* current record address */
int mbr_file;                         /* member.dat fd */
struct mbr_rcd hold_rcd;              /* hold area for member.dat record */
VOID get_rcd(), rtn_rcd(), gt_nxt(), clr_rcd(), gt_prv();
int tree;

 main()
 {
     static char term = '\0', c;

     setmem(&mbr_data, sizeof mbr_data, '\0');
     tree = init_b("mbrno.ndx", 5);
     read_screens("video.crt");
     if ((mbr_file = opn_file("members.dat", 0)) == ERROR)
         mbr_file = opn_file("members.dat", sizeof(mbr_data));
     clr_rcd();
     while (term != ESC)   {
         term = scrn_proc(1, mbr, FALSE);
         switch (term)       {
             case F10:              /* --- Next Record --- */
                 rtn_rcd();
                 gt_nxt();
                 break;
             case F9:               /* --- Previous Record --- */
                 rtn_rcd();
                 gt_prv();
                 break;
             case F7:               /* --- Delete Record --- */
                 if (existing_record)   {
                     err_msg("Verify delete with F7");
                     if ((c = get_byte()) == F7) {
                         delete_record(mbr_file, adr);
                         delete_key(tree, hold_rcd.mbr_no, adr);
                         clr_rcd();
                         adr = 0;
                         clrmsg();
```

Listing 12-1 (continued)

```
                    }
                    else
                        notice("Delete cancelled    ");
                }
                break;
            case GO:                /*-- Write Record --*/
                rtn_rcd();
                clr_rcd();
                break;
        }
    }
    clr_scrn();
    close_b(tree);
    cls_file(mbr_file);
    reset_screens();
    exit(0);
}

/* ------ called when member number is entered ------ */

int mbr_edit(mno,ky)
char *mno, ky;
{
    register int i;

    if (ky == ESC || ky == F9 || ky == F10 || ky == F7 || ky == GO)
        return OK;
    if (*mno == ' ')      {
        err_msg("Membership number required");
        return ERROR;
    }
    if (find_key(tree, mno, &adr))  {
        get_rcd();
        for (i = 1; i <= 10; i++)
            backfill(1, i, mbr);
    }
    else    {
        notice("New record being added");
        existing_record = FALSE;
    }
    return OK;
}

/* ----- return a record to the file or create a new one ----- */

VOID rtn_rcd()
{
    int i = sizeof(mbr_data);
    register char *s = mbr_data.mbr_no;
    register char *d = hold_rcd.mbr_no;

    if (existing_record)     {
```

Listing 12-1 (continued)

```
        while (i)                       /* test for record changed */
            if (*s++ != *d++)
                break;
            else
                i--;
        if (!i)
            return;
        notice("Changed record written to file");
        put_record(mbr_file, adr, &mbr_data);
    }
    else    {
        while (i)                       /* test for any data in rcd */
            if (*s == ' ' || *s == '\0')    {
                s++;
                i--;
            }
            else
                break;
        if (!i)
            return;
        notice("New record written to file");
        adr = new_record(mbr_file, &mbr_data);
        insert_key(tree,mbr_data.mbr_no,adr,TRUE);
    }

/* ----- save the new record in the hold area ----- */

    movmem(&mbr_data, &hold_rcd, sizeof(mbr_data));
}

/* ----- clear the record space ----- */

VOID clr_rcd()
{
    existing_record = FALSE;
    setmem(&mbr_data, sizeof(mbr_data), ' ');
    setmem(&hold_rcd, sizeof(mbr_data), ' ');
    mbr [0].protect = FALSE;
}


/* ------ get a record from the file ------ */

VOID get_rcd()
{
    existing_record = TRUE;
    get_record(mbr_file, adr, &mbr_data);
    movmem(&mbr_data, &hold_rcd, sizeof(mbr_data));
    mbr [0].protect = TRUE;
}


/* ----- get the next record from the file ----- */

VOID gt_nxt()
```

Listing 12-1 (continued)

```
e)) == (ADDR) NULL)
e");



cord from the file ----- */



== (ADDR) NULL)
file");


/* ------ help function for the membership number ------ */

char *mbr_help()
{
    notice("Enter the membership number of the member");
    return "\0";
}

/* ------ edit the membership type ------ */

int mbr_ty_edit(ty,ky)
char *ty, ky;
{
    *ty = toupper(*ty);
    switch (*ty)    {
        case ' ':
        case 'A':
        case 'L':
        case 'S':
```

Listing 12-1 (continued)

```
        return OK;
    default:
        err_msg("Invalid Membership Type");
        return ERROR;
    }
}
```

Figure 12-1 is a block diagram of the steps involved in using screen, file, and B-tree management, and "example.c" follows this pattern.

"Example.c" is a small membership recording program that might be used by any business or organization that needs to keep a file of its members. The file, called "members.dat," can be created by this program and records can be added to it. It uses the membership number as the indexed key to the file. The program can also be used to retrieve the record of any member on the basis of the membership number key. Selected records can be modified or deleted.

"Example.c" depends upon a screen definition file, video.crt," shown here as Figure 12-2. You build it with your screen or text editor just as we discussed in Chapter 9. If you remember the discussion about building these files in Chapter 9, you realize that you have quite a bit of latitude in the content of this file. It is only required that the data items on the screen, as represented by the strings of underlines, appear in their original sequence as shown in "video.crt". You can rearrange anything else on the screen. For example, you may want to put a banner showing the name of the organization at the top of the screen.

The program includes a file called "member.h." This is the same file used in the "sortexmp.c" and "sorttest.c" programs, and a listing of it can be found in Chapter 10. It contains the structure that defines the format of the membership file.

Notice the initialization of the scrn_buf structure. By using white space, the elements of the array can be shown in columns thereby improving the legibility of the program. This is helpful during testing or modification of the program. You can look at

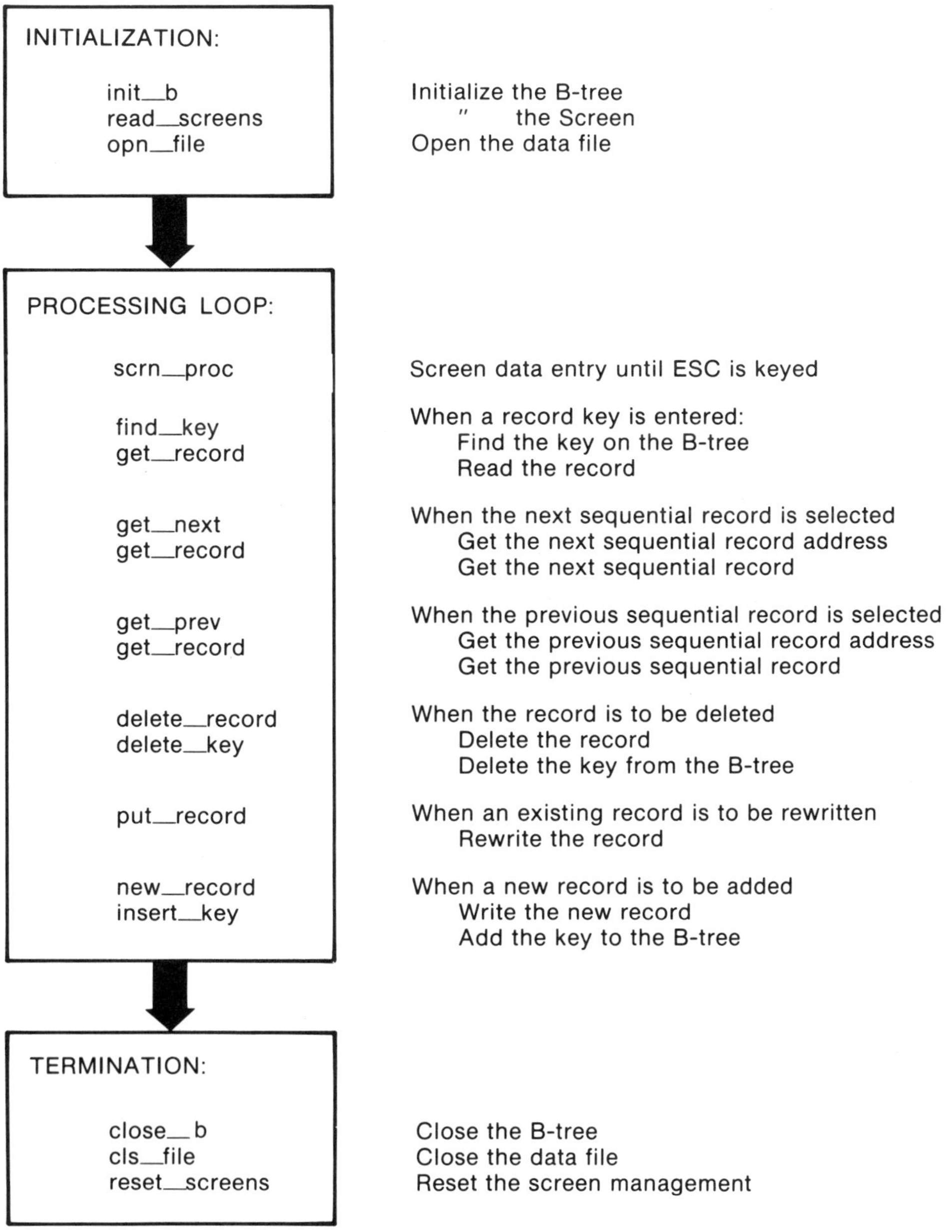

INITIALIZATION:

    init__b   Initialize the B-tree
    read__screens   "   the Screen
    opn__file   Open the data file

PROCESSING LOOP:

    scrn__proc   Screen data entry until ESC is keyed

    find__key   When a record key is entered:
    get__record   Find the key on the B-tree
                                    Read the record

    get__next   When the next sequential record is selected
    get__record   Get the next sequential record address
                                    Get the next sequential record

    get__prev   When the previous sequential record is selected
    get__record   Get the previous sequential record address
                                    Get the previous sequential record

    delete__record   When the record is to be deleted
    delete__key   Delete the record
                                    Delete the key from the B-tree

    put__record   When an existing record is to be rewritten
                                    Rewrite the record

    new__record   When a new record is to be added
    insert__key   Write the new record
                                    Add the key to the B-tree

TERMINATION:

    close__b   Close the B-tree
    cls__file   Close the data file
    reset__screens   Reset the screen management

**Figure 12-1. The steps involved in using screen,
file, and B-tree management.**

```
*

Member #:     ________
Name:         ________________________

Addr:         ________________________
              ________________________
City:         ________________________
St/Zip:       __  _____

Phone:        (__) __-___        Dues:  $_,___.__

Membership: [_]    (A = Annual, L = Lifetime, S = Special)
Exp. Date:    __/__/__
```

Figure 12-2. A screen definition file, video.crt.

the structure initialization and see how each data field on the screen is controlled.

The program begins by calling `init_b` to initialize the B-tree index file "mbrno.ndx". Then it calls `read_screens` to read in the file "video.crt." The file "members.dat" is opened if it exists. Otherwise it is created.

The program now enters a loop, calling `scrn_proc` to read in membership data. The loop continues until the user presses the ESCAPE key.

Each execution of `scrn_proc` displays the "video.crt" template, and the data values from whatever record in "members.dat" is currently in memory. Initially there is no record, so an empty template is shown, and the user must begin keying data. The first data field to be entered is the member number.

The function `mbr_edit` is called from inside the `scrn_proc` function when a member number has been keyed. `Mbr_edit` is a part of the "example.c" program and is called out in the `scrn_buf` structure as the function to call when the data element is keyed in. First it tests to see if a member number was entered. If no member number was entered, an error is posted. Otherwise, the B-tree function `find_key` is used to see if the member number is on the file. If so, the record is read and the data elements from it are written to the screen with the function `backfill`. If not, a notice is posted to tell the user that a new record is being added to the file.

Each call to `scrn_proc` returns the keystroke that the user used to complete the screen. The loop uses a **case** to properly process the keystroke.

In "example.c," function keys F9, F10 and F7 are used for the previous record, next record, and delete record processes, respectively. Each of these function keys causes `scrn_proc` to return to the "example.c" program. The keystroke called GO is also used by the `scrn_proc` function to indicate that entry is done, and it is used in "example.c" to write the current record to "members.dat" and start with an empty template again. For the IBM PC the GO key is assigned to F1. F9 and F10 (previous and next record command keys) write the current record to the file, but then retrieve the previous or next record, respectively, and proceed with data entry. Since the program is accessing the "members.dat" records by member number, the previous or next record processes use the B-tree functions `get_prev` and `get_next`. F7 is used to delete records from the file. Since you could press this key by accident, the program asks you to press it again to verify your meaning. If you do, the record being displayed is deleted from the file "members.dat" by using the file management function `delete_record` and the member number is deleted from the B-tree using the function `delete_key`.

Whenever a record is to be written to the "members.dat" file, the function `rtn_rcd` is used. This is a function in the program "example.c." If the record was already on file, and if the record has been changed by the user's data entry in `scrn_proc`, the file management function `put_record` is used. If it is a new record, the file management function `new_record` is used. This function returns a file address that must be inserted along with the member number into the B-tree. This insertion is done with the B-tree function `insert_key`.

When all processing is completed, the program calls `close_b` to close out the B-tree and `cls_file` to close the membership file.

The functions `mbr_help` and `mbr_ty_edit` illustrate how the caller-supplied help and edit functions work.

Summary

By combining "example.c" with "menuexmp.c" and "sortexmp.c," you can get a reasonably good understanding of how all the pieces of the toolset fit together. With the distribution of this collection, there is the potential for growth and expansion of these concepts. Using the functions in this book, and as important, the concepts of software development that are advanced by example and by practice, you enhance your software skills and, therefore, your productivity as a system designer and developer.

Appendices

The C Programmer's Workshop: C Language Source Code

Contents

```
/* --------------------- toolset.h --------------------- */

#define AZTEC_C86 1            /* Manx Aztec C86*/
#define LATTICE 2              /* Lattice C    */
#define CWARE 3                /* Cware DeSmet C*/
#define ECOC 4                 /* Eco-C88      */
#define MWC 5                  /* Mark Williams Let's C*/

#define COMPILER AZTEC_C86

#define ERROR -1
#define OK 0

#if COMPILER != ECOC
#define CMODE 0666
#define TRUE 1
#define FALSE 0
#endif

#if COMPILER == ECOC
#define CMODE 0
#endif

#if COMPILER == CWARE
#define O_RDONLY 0
#define O_WRONLY 1
#define O_RDWR   2
#endif

#if COMPILER == MWC
#define O_RDONLY 0
#define O_WRONLY 1
#define O_RDWR   2
#endif

#if COMPILER == LATTICE
#define VOID int
#else
#define VOID void
#endif

#define NODELEN 512    /* length of a Cache and B-tree node    */
#define ADDR long      /* B-tree node and file address         */
```

Listing A-1.

```
/* --------------------- subs.c --------------------------- */
#include "toolset.h"

/* A utility routine which moves blocks of memory.  The routine tests for
   the direction of the move so that overlapping areas can be moved  */

VOID movmem(s, d, l)
char *s, *d;
int l;
{
    if (d > s)
        while (l--)
            *(d + l) = *(s + l);
    else
        while (l--)
            *d++ = *s++;
}

/* A utility routine which sets every byte in a specified block of memory
   to a specified value */

VOID setmem(s, l, n)
char *s, n;
int l;
{
    while (l--)
        *s++ = n;
}

/* ------------- Fatal error --------------------------- */
VOID fatal(n)
int n;
{
    static char *errm [] = {"Insufficient memory for cache",
                            "Disk i/o error",
                            "Index file not properly closed",
                            "Cannot find template file",
                            "Insufficient memory for screens",
                            "Cannot find program",
                            "Screen buffer is too small",
                            "Insufficient memory for files",
                            "Insufficient memory for B-trees"};

    printf("\nError ts%03d: %s\nTerminating.", n, errm [n-1]);
    exit();
}

/* ------------ Execute a "child" process and return its return value ----- */
int execute(p, arg1, arg2)
char *p, *arg1, *arg2;
{
#if COMPILER == CWARE
    char tail [15];
    sprintf(tail, " %s %s", arg1, arg2);
    return exec(p, tail);
#endif
```

Listing A-2.

Listing A-2 (continued)

```
#if COMPILER == AZTEC_C86
    fexecl(p, p, arg1, arg2, 0);
    return wait();
#endif
#if COMPILER == LATTICE
    forkl(p, p, arg1, arg2, 0);
    return wait();
#endif
#if COMPILER == ECOC
    char tail [15];
    struct {
        unsigned es, cs, ss, ds;
    } seg;
    struct {
        unsigned env;
        char *cmd, *cmdds;
        char *of1, *os1, *of2, *os2;
    } pt;
    segread(&seg);
    pt.of1 = pt.of2 = pt.os1 = pt.os2 = (char *)0;
    sprintf(tail, " %s %s", arg1, arg2);
    pt.cmd = tail;
    pt.cmdds = (char *)seg.ds;
    pt.env = peek(seg.cs-0x10, 0x2c);
    return loadexec(p, seg.ds, &pt, seg.ds, 0);
#endif
#if COMPILER == MWC
    char tail [15];
    int rtn;
    sprintf(tail, " %s %s", arg1, arg2);
    rtn = execall(p, tail);
    return rtn == 63 ? ERROR : rtn;
#endif
}

#if COMPILER == LATTICE
#include <ctype.h>
/* ------------- Ascii to long function ------------ */
long atol(s)
char *s;
{
    long n = 0;
    char sign;

    while(*s == ' ' || *s == '\t')
        s++;
    sign = *s;
    if (*s == '-' || *s == '+')
        s++;
    while (isdigit (*s))
        n = n * 10 + (*s++ - '0');
    return sign == '-' ? -n : n;
}
#endif
```

```
/* -------------------- terminal.h -------------------- */

VOID init_crt();         /*   Initialize the terminal        */
int get_byte();          /*   Get a byte from the keyboard   */
VOID put_byte();         /*   Put a byte to the screen       */
VOID cursor();           /*   Set the cursor                 */
VOID high_intensity();   /*   Set intensity on/off           */
VOID underline();        /*   Set underline on/off           */
VOID clr_scrn();         /*   Clear the screen    */


/* -------------------- keys.h -------------------- */

/* Keyboard input values as returned by get_byte function in terminal.c.
   The values UP and FWD can be sent to put_byte to move the cursor.
   The value BELL can be sent to put_byte to ring the bell.  */

#define HELP 2         /*  help key                          */
#define DELETE 23      /*  delete character under cursor      */
#define GO 1           /*  GO key signals screen entry completed */
#define INSERT 22      /*  toggle insert mode on and off      */
#define UP 11          /*  cursor up                         */
#define RUBOUT 127     /*  delete character to left of cursor  */
#define DITTO 3        /*  user ditto key                    */
#define ESC 27         /*  escape key                        */
#define FWD 12         /*  cursor one space to right         */
#define F1 1           /*  function key                      */
#define F2 2           /*  function key                      */
#define F3 3           /*  function key                      */
#define F4 4           /*  function key                      */
#define F5 5           /*  function key                      */
#define F6 6           /*  function key                      */
#define F7 7           /*  function key                      */
#define F8 18          /*  function key                      */
#define F9 29          /*  function key                      */
#define F10 20         /*  function key                      */
               /*  other values (backspace, line feed, etc.)
                   use C conventions (/b, /n, etc.)  */
#define BELL 7         /*  terminal audible alarm output value  */
#define HT 8           /*  spacing for the horizontal tab       */
```

Listing A-3.

```
/* ----------------------- terminal.c ------------------------------- */

/* ------ Terminal dependent functions.
    These are coded for the IBM PC with ANSI.SYS ---- */
#include <stdio.h>
#include "toolset.h"
#include "keys.h"
#include "terminal.h"

#define COLOR

#if COMPILER == AZTEC_C86        /* Aztec C86 for MS-DOS */
#define getchar() bdos(7,0,0)
#define putchar(c) bdos(2,c,0)
#endif

#if COMPILER == LATTICE          /* Lattice and Microsoft C */
#define getchar() getch()
#define putchar(c) putch(c)
#endif

#if COMPILER == CWARE            /* DeSmet CWARE C */
#define getchar() ci()
#define putchar(c) co(c)
#endif

#if COMPILER == ECOC             /* Eco-C88 */
#define getchar() getch()
#define putchar(c) _putc(c,stdout)
#endif

#if COMPILER == MWC              /* Let's C */
#define getchar() getcnb()
#define putchar(c) putcnb(c)
#endif

int curr_crt = 0;        /* current screen template */
int under_ = 0;          /* underline mode */
int high_ = 0;           /* high intensity mode */

#define SVDEPTH 10

/* pseudo stack for nested levels of graphics renditions */

int sv_ints [SVDEPTH], sv_und [SVDEPTH], svp = 0;
VOID sgr(), save_gr(), rstr_gr();

/* ---------------- initialize the terminal ------------------- */

VOID init_crt()
{
    static int initd = FALSE;
```

Listing A-4.

Listing A-4 (continued)

```
    if (initd)
        return;
    initd = TRUE;
    under_ = high_ = svp = 0;
    sgr();
/* clr_scrn(); */
}


/* -------- Keyboard input routine. ------------------------------- */

int get_byte()
{
    int c;
    register int i;
    static char kys [] = ";(=)?@ABCDGHIKMOPQRS";
    static int cc [] = {F1,F2,F3,F4,F5,F6,F7,F8,F9,F10,0,UP,0,'\b',
                        FWD,0,'\n',0,INSERT,DELETE};
#if COMPILER == MWC
    fflush(stdout);
#endif
    if (!(c = getchar()))   {               /* first byte = null means func key */
        c = getchar();                      /* second byte of function key */
        for (i = 0; i < sizeof kys; i++)    /* translate to */
            if (c == kys [i])               /* Workshop value */
                return cc [i];
    }
    if (c == 8)                             /* use back space key for rubout */
        c = RUBOUT;
    return c;
}


/* ---------- set intensity ------------------ */

VOID high_intensity(i)
int i;
{
    high_ = i;
    sgr();
}


/* ---------- set underline -------------------- */

VOID underline(u)
int u;
{
    under_ = u;
    sgr();
}

/* ------------ set graphics rendition -------------------- */

VOID sgr()
```

Listing A-4 (continued)

```
{
#ifdef COLOR
    static char *c[] = {"[0m", "[0m", "[0;1m", "[0;1m"};
#else
    static char *c[] = {"[0m", "[0;4m", "[0;1m", "[1;4m"};
#endif
    register char *p;

    p = c [high_ * 2 + under_];    /* ANSI.SYS values for intensity, */
    put_byte(ESC);                 /* and underline modes */
    while (*p)
        put_byte(*p++);
}


/* -------- save the graphics rendition ---------------- */

VOID save_gr()
{
    if (svp < SVDEPTH) {           /* put the latest modes in a lifo */
        sv_ints [svp] = high_;
        sv_und [svp++] = under_;
    }
}


/* -------- restore the graphics rendition ---------------- */

VOID rstr_gr()
{
    if (svp)    {                  /* get the modes from the lifo */
        high_ = sv_ints [--svp];
        under_ = sv_und [svp];
        sgr();                     /* set the rendition */
    }
}

/* ----------Terminal output routine. ---------------- */
VOID put_byte(c)
int c;
{
#if COMPILER == MWC
    fflush(stdout);
#endif
    if (c == '\n')                 /* line feed = carr rtn, line feed */
        putchar('\r');
    if (c == FWD)    {             /* ANSI.SYS cursor -} */
        putchar(ESC);
        putchar('[');
        putchar('C');
    }
    else if (c == UP)    {         /* ANSI.SYS cursor ^ */
        putchar(ESC);
```

Listing A-4 (continued)

```
        putchar('[');
        putchar('A');
    }
    else    {
#ifdef COLOR
        if (c == ' ' && under_)
            c = '_';
#endif
        putchar(c);
    }
}


/* ---------------- Put the cursor at screen location x/y -------------- */
VOID cursor(x,y)
int x, y;
{
    x++;
    y++;
    put_byte(ESC);                      /* ANSI.SYS cursor position protocol */
    put_byte('[');
    put_byte(y / 10 + 0x30);
    put_byte(y % 10 + 0x30);
    put_byte(';');
    put_byte(x / 10 + 0x30);
    put_byte(x % 10 + 0x30);
    put_byte('H');
}


/* ------------------ clear the screen ------------------------- */
VOID clr_scrn()
{
    put_byte(ESC);                      /* ANSI.SYS clear screen */
    put_byte('[');
    put_byte('2');
    put_byte('J');
    curr_crt = 0;
}
```

```
/* --------------------- cache.h -------------------- */

VOID init_cache();      /*     Initializes the Cache buffers    */
char *get_node();       /*     Gets a node from Cache           */
VOID put_node();        /*     Puts a node to Cache             */
VOID release_node();    /*     Releases a node to Cache         */
VOID flush_cache();     /*     Flushes the Cache buffers        */
```

Listing A-5.

```
/* -------------------------------- cache.c ------------------------------------- */

#include (stdio.h)
#include "toolset.h"

#define MXNODES 25      /* number of cache nodes to be supported  */
#define FREE 0          /* list head subscript globals */
#define INUSE 1
#define RELEASED 2

VOID add_node(), remove_node();



/* -------------------- Cache Nodes -------------------- */

struct cnode   {
    struct cnode *nxt_out;  /* Pointer to next node in the list  */
    struct cnode *prev_out; /* Pointer to previous node in the list  */
    int nd_chgd;            /* 0 = data not changed between get_node
                                and release_node.
                             1 = data changed by caller  */
    char *n_ptr;            /* points to data space of node  */
    ADDR nd_sector;         /* relative sector within file  */
    int nd_fd;              /* fd of file that node goes with  */
    } nodes_in [MXNODES];   /* one of these for each node  */


/* ---------------- Cache Linked List Heads ---------------------- */

struct  {
    struct cnode *first_out;    /* Pointer to first node on list  */
    struct cnode *last_out;     /* Pointer to last node on list */
    } list_head [3];            /* There are 3 lists:
                                    0 = free nodes;
                                    1 = nodes in use by caller;
                                    2 = nodes released by caller */

struct cnode *new_node(), *lru();
int cache_init = FALSE;

/* -------------------- Initialize the Cache structures --------------- */

VOID init_cache()
{
    register int i;
    char *malloc();

    if (cache_init)
        return;         /* --- already initialized --- */
    cache_init = TRUE;
```

Listing A-6.

Listing A-6 (continued)

```
/* ---- build the linked list listhead ---- */

list_head [FREE].first_out = &nodes_in [0];      /* free -> 1st node */
list_head [FREE].last_out = &nodes_in [MXNODES-1]; /* free -> last node */
for (i = 1; i < 3; i++) {
    list_head [i].first_out = NULL; /* released and in-use -> nowhere */
    list_head [i].last_out = NULL;  /*    "      "     "    "     "     */
}

/* ---- initialize the nodes in the linked list ------ */

for (i = 0; i < MXNODES; i++)   {
    nodes_in [i].nxt_out = &nodes_in [i + 1];   /* this one -> next one */
    nodes_in [i].prev_out = i ? &nodes_in [i - 1] : NULL;  /* -> prior one */
    nodes_in [i].nd_chgd = FALSE;               /* unchanged */
    if (!(nodes_in [i].n_ptr = malloc(NODELEN)))/* space for a node */
        fatal(1);
    nodes_in [i].nd_sector = 0;                 /* no sector in this node */
    nodes_in [i].nd_fd = NULL;                  /* no file for this node */
    setmem(nodes_in [i].n_ptr, NODELEN, '\0');
}
nodes_in [MXNODES-1].nxt_out = NULL;            /* last node -> nowhere */
}

/* ------ Get the node p from fd. Return a pointer to the data ------- */

char *get_node(fd, p)
int fd;
ADDR p;
{
    long sect;
    register struct cnode *cn;

    /* ---- search released nodes for a match on the requested node ---- */

    cn = list_head [RELEASED].first_out;
    while (cn != NULL) {
        if (cn->nd_sector == p && cn->nd_fd == fd){
            remove_node(RELEASED, cn);      /* remove node from released */
            add_node(INUSE, cn);            /* add node to in use list */
            return (cn->n_ptr);
        }
        cn = cn->nxt_out;
    }

    /* ---- get a node from the free list or get a released one ----*/

    cn = new_node(INUSE, fd, p);

    /* ---- read in the data for the node ---- */

    sect = p - 1;
```

Listing A-6 (continued)

```
    sect *= NODELEN;
    if (lseek(fd, sect, 0) == ERROR)
        setmem(cn->n_ptr, NODELEN, '\0');
    else if (read(fd, cn->n_ptr, NODELEN) == ERROR)
        fatal(2);
    cn->nd_chgd = FALSE;
    return (cn->n_ptr);
}
/* ------- put a new record into Cache from the caller's buffer --------- */

VOID put_node(fd,t,buff)
int fd;
ADDR t;
char *buff;
{
    register struct cnode *cn;

    /* ---- search released nodes for a match on the requested node ---- */

    cn = list_head [RELEASED].first_out;
    while (cn != NULL)  {
        if (cn->nd_sector == t && cn->nd_fd == fd)
            break;
        cn = cn->nxt_out;
    }

    /* -- if the node is not in the released list, appropriate a new one --- */

    if (cn == NULL)
        cn = new_node(RELEASED,fd,t);
    cn->nd_chgd = TRUE;
    movmem(buff,cn->n_ptr,NODELEN);
}

/* -------------- appropriate a new node --------------- */

struct cnode *new_node(list,fd,t)
int list,fd;
ADDR t;
{
    register struct cnode *cn;

    if ((cn = list_head [FREE].first_out) != NULL){
        remove_node(FREE, cn);      /* --- get a free node --- */
        add_node(list, cn);
    }
    else
        cn = lru(list);             /* -- get the least recently used node - */
    cn->nd_sector = t;
    cn->nd_fd = fd;
    return (cn);
}
```

Listing A-6 (continued)

```
/* ------------- release node p to the Cache process -------------- */

VOID release_node(fd,p,chgd)
int fd,chgd;
ADDR p;
{
    register struct cnode *cn;

    cn = list_head [INUSE].first_out;
    while (cn != NULL)  {
        if (cn->nd_sector == p && cn->nd_fd == fd){
            cn->nd_chgd != chgd;
            remove_node(INUSE, cn);
            add_node(RELEASED, cn);
            return;
        }
        cn = cn->nxt_out;
    }
}

/* ----- Flush data from the Cache structures. Called when either a file
     is to be closed or to clear out all buffers for safe-keeping ---------- */

VOID flush_cache(fd)
int fd;
{
    register struct cnode *cn, *J;
    long sect;
    int i;

    cn = list_head [RELEASED].first_out;
    while (cn != NULL)  {
        J = cn->nxt_out;
        if (fd == cn->nd_fd || !fd) {
            if (cn->nd_chgd)     {
                sect = cn->nd_sector-1;
                sect *= NODELEN;
                lseek(fd, sect, 0);
                write(fd, cn->n_ptr, NODELEN);
            }
            cn->nd_chgd = FALSE;
            cn->nd_sector = 0;
            cn->nd_fd = 0;
            remove_node(RELEASED, cn);
            add_node(FREE, cn);
        }
        cn = J;
    }
    if (!fd)     {
        cache_init = FALSE;
        for (i = 0; i < MXNODES; i++)
            free(nodes_in [i].n_ptr);
    }
```

```
}


/* ------- Send least recently used node to disk if it has been changed.
      Put it into the specified list.  Return the offset to it. ---------- */
struct cnode *lru(list)
int list;
{
    register struct cnode *cn;
    long sect;

    cn = list_head [RELEASED].first_out;
    if (cn->nd_chgd)      {
        sect = cn->nd_sector - 1;
        sect *= NODELEN;
        lseek(cn->nd_fd, sect, 0);
        write(cn->nd_fd, cn->n_ptr, NODELEN);
    }
    remove_node(RELEASED, cn);
    add_node(list, cn);
    return (cn);
}
/* -------------------- Add a node to a list -------------------- */

VOID add_node(list,n_node)
int list;
struct cnode *n_node;
{
    if (list_head [list].first_out == NULL)
        list_head [list].first_out = n_node;
    if (list_head [list].last_out != NULL)
        list_head [list].last_out->nxt_out = n_node;
    n_node->prev_out = list_head [list].last_out;
    list_head [list].last_out = n_node;
    n_node->nxt_out = NULL;
}




/* -------------- remove a node from the list it is in ---------------- */
VOID remove_node(list_no, n_node)
int list_no;
struct cnode *n_node;
{
    if (list_head [list_no].first_out == n_node)
        list_head [list_no].first_out = n_node->nxt_out;
    else
        (n_node->prev_out)->nxt_out = n_node->nxt_out;
    if (list_head [list_no].last_out == n_node)
        list_head [list_no].last_out = n_node->prev_out;
```

Listing A-6 (continued)

```
else
     (n_node->nxt_out)->prev_out = n_node->prev_out;
n_node->nxt_out = NULL;
n_node->prev_out = NULL;
}
```

```
/* ----------------------- file.h ------------------------------ */

/* file management function declarations */

int opn_file();          /*    Opens a data file                 */
VOID cls_file();         /*    Closes a data file                */
ADDR new_record();       /*    Adds a record to a file           */
int delete_record();     /*    Deletes a record from a file      */
int get_record();        /*    Gets a record from a file         */
int put_record();        /*    Puts a record to a file           */
```

Listing A-7.

```
/* ----------------------- filhdr.h ----------------------- */

/* The format for the header record at the beginning of a Toolset file */

struct fil_hdr  {        /* header on each file */
    ADDR fst_rcd;        /* first available deleted record */
    ADDR nxt_rcd;        /* next available record position */
    int rcd_len;         /* length of record */
};
```

Listing A-8.

```
/* ----------------------- files.c ------------------------------ */

#include <stdio.h>
#include "toolset.h"
#if COMPILER != CWARE
#if COMPILER != MWC
#include <fcntl.h>
#endif
#endif
#include "filhdr.h"
#include "file.h"
#include "cache.h"

#define MAXFILES 10          /* maximum random files per calling program */

int r_len [MAXFILES];        /* record lengths */
int f_fd [MAXFILES];         /* file descriptors */
ADDR nxav [MAXFILES];        /* next available file addresses */
int fp = 0;                  /* points to next available file slot */
VOID locate(), new_file();

/* --------- returns the length of a record in the file fd ----------- */

int rcd_length(fd)
int fd;
{
    return (fd > MAXFILES || !f_fd [fd]) ? ERROR : r_len [fd];
}

/* -------------- called to open a random file ---------------- */

int opn_file(name, len)
char *name;
int len;
{
    register struct fil_hdr *b;

    if (fp == MAXFILES)
        return ERROR;
    init_cache();
    if (len)   {                            /* len > 0 = create the file */
        f_fd [fp] = creat(name, CMODE);
        close(f_fd [fp]);
        f_fd [fp] = open(name, O_RDWR);
        new_file(len);
    }
    else
        if ((f_fd [fp] = open(name, O_RDWR)) == ERROR)
            return ERROR;
    b = (struct fil_hdr *) get_node(f_fd [fp], (ADDR) 1); /* file header */
    r_len [fp] = b->rcd_len;                      /* save record length */
```

Listing A-9.

Listing A-9 (continued)

```
    nxav [fp] = b->nxt_rcd;                          /* pointer to last record+1*/
    release_node(f_fd [fp], (ADDR) 1, 0);
    return fp++;                                      /* return the file pointer */
}



/* -------------- called to close a random file ---------------- */
VOID cls_file(fd)
int fd;
{
    flush_cache(f_fd [fd]);
    close(f_fd [fd]);
    f_fd [fd] = 0;
}

/* -- called to initialize new file with free space listhead in 1st sector - */
VOID new_file(len)
int len;
{
    register struct fil_hdr *b;

    b = (struct fil_hdr *) get_node(f_fd [fp], (ADDR) 1); /* file header */
    b->nxt_rcd = 1;                                  /* next record address */
    b->fst_rcd = 0;                                  /* 1st deleted record address*/
    b->rcd_len = len;                                /* record length */
    release_node(f_fd [fp], (ADDR) 1, 1);
}



/* ----- called to create a new record. Returns the record number ------ */

ADDR new_record(fd, buff)
int fd;
char *buff;
{
    ADDR rcd_no;
    char *malloc();
    register struct fil_hdr *r, *c;

    r = (struct fil_hdr *) get_node(f_fd [fd], (ADDR) 1); /* file header  */
    if (r->fst_rcd) {                                /* any deleted rcds to reuse?*/
        rcd_no = r->fst_rcd;                         /* yes, use the deleted one */
        if (!(c = (struct fil_hdr *) malloc(r_len [fd])))
            fatal(8);
        release_node(f_fd [fd], (ADDR) 1, 0);
        get_record(fd, rcd_no, c);       /* get the old copy of it */
        r = (struct fil_hdr *) get_node(f_fd [fd], (ADDR) 1); /* file header  */
        r->fst_rcd = c->nxt_rcd;                     /* put its nxt into hdrs 1st */
        free(c);
    }
```

Listing A-9 (continued)

```
    else    {                               /* no deleted rcds to reuse */
        rcd_no = r->nxt_rcd++;              /* record number */
        nxav [fd] = rcd_no + 1;             /* set next available */
    }
    release_node(f_fd [fd], (ADDR) 1, 1);
    put_record(fd, rcd_no, buff);           /* put the new record */
    return rcd_no;
}


/* -------------- called to delete an existing record --------------- */

int delete_record(fd, rcd_no)
int fd;
ADDR rcd_no;
{
    register struct fil_hdr *b, *buff;
    char *malloc();

    if (rcd_no > nxav [fd])
        return ERROR;                       /* non-existing record */
    if (!(buff = (struct fil_hdr *) malloc(r_len [fd])))
        fatal(8);
    setmem(buff, r_len [fd], '\0');
    b = (struct fil_hdr *) get_node(f_fd [fd], (ADDR) 1);/* file header  */
    buff->nxt_rcd = b->fst_rcd;             /* point deleted rcd to nxt */
    buff->fst_rcd = (-1);                   /* mark record deleted */
    b->fst_rcd = rcd_no;                    /* point hdr to deleted rcd */
    release_node(f_fd [fd], (ADDR) 1, 1);
    put_record(fd, rcd_no, buff);
    free(buff);
    return OK;
}


/* ---------------- called to retrieve an existing record -------------- */

int get_record(fd, rcd_no, buff)
int fd;
ADDR rcd_no;
char *buff;
{
    int pos, d, len;
    ADDR sector;
    register char *d_ptr;
    register struct fil_hdr *b;

    if (rcd_no >= nxav [fd])
        return ERROR;                       /* record doesn't exist */
    len = r_len [fd];
    locate(rcd_no, len, &sector, &pos); /* compute sector, position */

    while (len) {
```

Listing A-9 (continued)

```
        d_ptr = get_node(f_fd [fd], sector);     /* read nth sector */
        for (d = pos; d ( NODELEN && len; d++)  {
            *buff++ = *(d_ptr + d);              /* move data to caller*/
            len--;
        }
        release_node(f_fd [fd], sector, 0);
        pos = 0;
        sector++;
    }
    return OK;
}


/* ---------------- called to rewrite an existing record ------------- */

int put_record(fd, rcd_no, buff)
int fd;
ADDR rcd_no;
char *buff;
{
    int pos, d, len;
    ADDR sector;
    register char *d_ptr;

    if (rcd_no ) nxav [fd])
        return ERROR;
    len = r_len [fd];
    locate(rcd_no, len, &sector, &pos); /* compute sector, position */

    while (len) {
        d_ptr = get_node(f_fd [fd], sector);
        for (d = pos; d ( NODELEN && len; d++)  {
            *(d_ptr + d) = *buff++;            /* move data from caller*/
            len--;
        }
        release_node(f_fd [fd], sector, 1);
        pos = 0;
        sector++;
    }
    return OK;
}


/* ------ compute sector and byte position from record number and length --- */

VOID locate(rcd_no, len, sector, pos)
int len, *pos;
ADDR rcd_no, *sector;
{
    long byte_ct;
```

Listing A-9 (continued)

```
    byte_ct = rcd_no - 1;
    byte_ct *= len;
    byte_ct += (sizeof(ADDR) * 2) + sizeof(int);
    *sector = (ADDR) (byte_ct / NODELEN + 1);
    *pos = (int) (byte_ct % NODELEN);
}
```

```
/* ------------------- menu.h -------------------------- */

#define MXSELS 10          /* maximum selections on a menu */

struct mif                 /* the structure which describes a menu */
    {
    char *m_title;         /* menu title       */
    char *keytab;          /* pointer to keystroke table */
    struct {
        char *m_sel;       /* text of selection */
        int m_vector;      /* vector to new menu */
        int (*func)();     /* pointer to function */
        char *pname;       /* name of program to execute */
        } sels [MXSELS];
    };

VOID menu_exec();          /*    Executes the menu         */
```

Listing A-10.

```c
/* ---------------------- menu.c ---------------------------- */

#include <stdio.h>
#include "toolset.h"
#if COMPILER != CWARE
#include <ctype.h>
#endif
#include "menu.h"
#include "terminal.h"
#include "keys.h"

#define DEPTH 25        /* Menu retreat depth */
#define HEIGHT 24       /* Number of lines per screen */
#define WIDTH 80        /* Number of characters per screen line */

int curr_mif = 0;       /* current menu in force */
int menu_up = 0;        /* indicates menu displayed */
VOID menu();

VOID menu_exec(mp, cm, s, banner)
int cm;                 /* menu to start with */
int s;                  /* forced 1st selection or NULL for menu display*/
struct mif *mp;         /* menu array pointer */
int (*banner)();        /* pointer to caller's banner writer */
{
    register struct mif *mf;        /* menu in force pointer */
    int (*ff)();                    /* function pointer  */
    int stack [DEPTH];              /* menu depth stack */
    char *sttitle [DEPTH];          /* menu titles on stack */
    int sp = 0;                     /* stack pointer */
    static char ccm [3] = "00";     /* string of menu number */
    static char cs [3] = "00";      /* string of selection */
    register char *p;

    curr_mif = cm;
    while (TRUE)    {
        while (s != ESC)    {
            mf = mp + curr_mif - 1;
            if (!s) {

                /* ---- selection == 0 ----- */

                menu(mf, banner);
                printf("ESC to return to %s", curr_mif == 1 ? "DOS" :
                    curr_mif == cm ? mp->m_title : sttitle [sp]);
                s = menu_sel(mf);
            }
            else if (mf->sels [s - 1].func) {

                /* --- this selection is a function call --- */
```

Listing A-11.

```
                menu_up = FALSE;
                ff = mf->sels [s - 1].func;
                s = (*ff)(curr_mif, s);
            }
            else if (mf->sels [s - 1].pname [0]){

                /* ---- this selection is an external program --- */

                menu_up = FALSE;
                cursor(0, HEIGHT - 2);
                p = mf->sels [s - 1].pname;
                printf("Loading %s...", p);
#if COMPILER == MWC
                fflush(stdout);
#endif
                sprintf(ccm, "%02d", curr_mif);
                sprintf(cs, "%02d", s);
                s = execute(p, ccm, cs);
                if (s == ERROR)
                    fatal(6);
            }
            else    {

            /* --- this selection is a new menu in force --- */

                if (sp == DEPTH)
                    sp = (-1);
                sttitle [++sp] = mf->m_title;
                stack [sp] = curr_mif;
                curr_mif = mf->sels [s - 1].m_vector;
                s = 0;
            }
        }

        /* --- ESCAPE was selected --- */

        s = 0;
        if (curr_mif == 1)
            break;                          /* --- at top level menu, quit --- */
        else if (curr_mif == cm)    {
            sp = 0;                         /* --- retreat from here to top level menu --- */
            curr_mif = 1;
        }
        else    {

            /* --- retreat to prior menu --- */

            curr_mif = stack [sp--];
            if (sp == (-1))
                sp = DEPTH;
        }
    }
}
```

Listing A-11 (continued)

```
    clr_scrn();
}

/* ----------------- Display a menu ---------------------- */

VOID menu(mf, banner)
struct mif *mf;        /* pointer to menu to display */
int (*banner)();       /* pointer to caller's banner writer */
{
    register int i, j;
    static int tln, tlc, tll, sll, jll;

    j = menu_height(mf);
    if (!menu_up)   {                    /* --- no menu is on the screen --- */
        clr_scrn();
        if (banner)                      /* --- caller's banner writer --- */
            (*banner)(curr_mif);
    }
    else    {                            /* --- a menu is on the screen --- */
        cursor(tlc, tll);
        while (tln--)
            putchar(' ');                /* --- clear the old title --- */
        for (i = 0; i (= jll; i++)  {
            cursor(WIDTH/4, sll + i);    /* --- clear the selections --- */
            printf("                                     ");
        }
    }
    tln = strlen(mf->m_title);
    tlc = (WIDTH - 1 - tln) / 2;
    tll = (HEIGHT - 1 - j) / 2;
    sll = tll + 2;
    menu_up = TRUE;
    cursor(tlc, tll);
    printf(mf->m_title);                 /* --- display the title --- */
    for (i = 0; i ( MXSELS; i++)          {
        cursor(WIDTH / 4, sll + i);
        if (mf->sels [i].m_sel == (char *) NULL)
            break;
        else
            printf(mf->sels [i].m_sel); /* --- display selections --- */
    }
    jll = i + 2;
}

/* ------------- Compute height of menu text ---------------------- */

int menu_height(mf)
struct mif *mf;
{
    register int i;

    for (i = 0; i ( MXSELS; i++)
        if (!mf->sels [i].m_sel)
```

Listing A-11 (continued)

```
            break;
        return 4 + i;
}


/* ---------------- Get a user selection from a menu ---------------- */
int menu_sel(mf)
struct mif *mf;                    /* pointer to menu in force */
{
    int j;                         /* maximum selections allowed + 4 */
    register int i;
    char c;
    int errup = 0;

    j = menu_height(mf);
    while (1)    {
        cursor(WIDTH / 4 + 3, (HEIGHT - 1 - j) / 2 + j);
        printf("Enter Selection [_]\b\b");
        c = get_byte();
        if (isprint(c))
            put_byte(c);
        if (errup) {
            errup = 0;                /* ---- clear the error line ---- */
            cursor(0, 0);
            printf("                    ");
        }
        if (c == ESC)
            return (int) c;
        if (!mf->keytab && c > '0' && c < j - 3 + '0')
            return (int) c - '0';        /* digit selections */
        else if (mf->keytab)             /* tabled selections */
            for (i = 0; i < j - 4; i++)
                if (tolower(c) == tolower(*(mf->keytab + i)))
                    return i + 1;
        cursor(0, 0);
        printf("Invalid Selection%c",7);
        errup++;
    }
}
```

```
/* -------------------- screen.h ------------------------ */

/*   This is the file of global symbols for the Toolset
     screen processes.              */

#define SCRNID '*'       /*  starts a screen template   */
#define SCBUFF 1920      /*  most characters needed for a screen   */
#define MAXSCRNS 5       /*  maximum screens allowed in a file   */
#define MAXFIELDS 30     /*  maximum fields on a screen   */
#define FLDFILL '_'      /*  field filler character   */

/*   This is the structure required to use the screen management functions.
     It is set up as an array with one entry per field on a screen.
     The calling program will initialize the array entries for each field.   */

struct scrn_buf {
    char item_type;      /*  'A' = alpha-numeric
                             'N' = numeric to be space filled
                             'Z' = numeric to be zero filled
                             'C' = currency
                             'D' = date         */
    int protect;         /* TRUE = protected field*/
    char *item_value;    /* pointer to string for data to be in  */
    int (*edits)();      /* pointer to edit function*/
    char *(*helps)();    /* pointer to help function*/
    int fill_data;       /* TRUE to backfill, FALSE to clear      */
    int ditto;           /* TRUE for automatic value ditto*/
    char *dit_ptr;       /* -) ditto value data space*/
};

/*   screen management function declarations   */

VOID read_screens();    /*    Reads screen definitions       */
char scrn_proc();       /*    Collects a screen of input data  */
VOID err_msg();         /*    Displays an error message      */
VOID notice();          /*    Displays a notice              */
VOID clrmsg();          /*    Clears the message/notice line   */
VOID backfill();        /*    Writes an item to the screen   */
char get_item();        /*    Reads an item from the screen   */
VOID reset_screens();   /*    Reset Screen Management system   */
```

Listing A-12.

```
/* ---------------------- screen.c --------------------------- */

#include (stdio.h)
#include "toolset.h"
#if COMPILER != CWARE
#include (ctype.h)
#endif
#include "screen.h"
#include "terminal.h"
#include "keys.h"

#define PADCHAR 26      /* padding character in an ASCII file */

struct {
    int no_flds;                    /* number of fields on the screen */
    char *s_mptr;                   /* pointer to screen image */
    struct {
        char *f_mptr;               /* points to field mask */
        int f_len;                  /* field length */
        int f_x;                    /* x cursor coordinate */
        int f_y;                    /* y cursor coordinate */
        int din;                    /* true = data has been entered*/
    } f_ [MAXFIELDS];               /* one per field */
    } s_ [MAXSCRNS];                /* one per screen */

int nbrcrts = 0;                    /* number of screens in the screen file */
int inserting = FALSE;              /* insert mode, TRUE or FALSE    */
int last_x = 0, last_y = 0;         /* current cursor location       */
extern int curr_crt;                /* current crt number */
int msg_up = FALSE;                 /* TRUE says message has been up */

char *find_field(), get_data();
VOID display_crt(), r_just(), z_just(), zl_just(), disp_fld(),
    insert_line(), save_gr(), rstr_gr();

/* ------ Read in the crt screens and save in memory. The caller passes the
   file name to the function. --------- */

VOID read_screens(screen_name)
char *screen_name;
{

    char *malloc();

    FILE *sc_file, *fopen();
    int x = 0, y = 0;
    int c;
    register char *scp = 0;
    int sc = 0;
    int fl = 0;
    char *cct;
```

Listing A-13.

Listing A-13 (continued)

```
            setmem(s_, sizeof s_, '\0');
init_crt();
if ((sc_file = fopen(screen_name, "r")) == NULL){
    printf("\n%s",screen_name);
    fatal(4);
}


/* ---- read in the file of screen templates and build field pointers --- */

while ((c = getc(sc_file)) != EOF && c != PADCHAR){
    switch (c)  {
        case SCRNID:                         /* screen id character */
            if (scp)       {                 /* if this is not the 1st */
                sc++;
                *scp = (char) c;
            }
            while ((c = getc(sc_file)) != '\n'/* bypass this line */
                    && c != EOF && c != PADCHAR)
                ;
            fl = 0;
            if ((cct = scp = malloc(SCBUFF)) == 0)/* get a screen buffer*/
                fatal(5);
            setmem(scp, SCBUFF, '\0');
            s_ [sc].s_mptr = scp;            /* point to buffer */
            x = 0;                           /* cursor xy */
            y = 0;
            break;
        case FLDFILL:                        /* field id character */
            s_ [sc].no_flds++;               /* count fields */
            s_ [sc].f_ [fl].f_mptr = scp;    /* point to mask */
            s_ [sc].f_ [fl].f_x = x;         /* save field xy */
            s_ [sc].f_ [fl].f_y = y;
            s_ [sc].f_ [fl].din = FALSE;     /* data indicator */
            while (c == FLDFILL || punct(c)){/* to end of field */
                if (c == FLDFILL)
                    s_ [sc].f_ [fl].f_len++;/* compute length */
                *scp++ = (char) c;           /* put mask into tem */
                x++;

                c = getc(sc_file);
            }
            *scp++ = '\0';                   /* null term at end of field */
            ungetc(c, sc_file);
            fl++;
            break;
        case '\n':
            x = 0;
            y++;
            *scp++ = (char) c;
            break;
```

Listing A-13 (continued)

```
            case '\t':
                x = ((x / HT) * HT) + HT;
                *scp++ = (char) c;
                break;
            default:                        /* displayable characters */
                if (isprint(c)) {
                    x++;
                    *scp++ = (char) c;
                }
                break;
        }

            if (scp > cct + SCBUFF)          /* template is too big */
                fatal(7);
        }
        fclose(sc_file);
        nbrcrts = sc;
        *scp = SCRNID;
}




/* ---- Reset screen management when through ------------- */

VOID reset_screens()
{
    while (nbrcrts != (-1))
        free(s_[nbrcrts--].s_mptr);
    underline(FALSE);
    high_intensity(FALSE);
}



/* ----- Process a screen of data.  Collect its item values into callers area.
    Input parameters:
            screen number (1-n)
            pointer to structure of screen data (see screen.h)
            go_last  = TRUE if screen is done upon CR or ENTER
                        for last field on screen.
                     = FALSE if GO button must be used to finish.
    The function returns the single character which terminated the last entry
    on the screen.  This is useful to see if the user used GO or ESCAPE. ---- */

char scrn_proc(scrn_no, scrn_data, go_last)
int scrn_no, go_last;
struct scrn_buf *scrn_data;
{
```

Listing A-13 (continued)

```
int (*edit_funct)();
char *(*help_funct)(), *char1, get_data();

struct scrn_buf *sb;
int i, fld, fld_ct, f, this_x, this_y;
int fld_ptr, done, len, edit_result;
char ex, prev = '\r';
register char *edit_mask, *bfptr;
char *find_field();

if (scrn_no != curr_crt)    {           /* display the template if */
    display_crt(scrn_no);               /* not already on the screen */
    curr_crt = scrn_no;
}

fld_ct = s_ [scrn_no-1].no_flds;        /* number of fields, this template */

/* ---- for each field, process ditto, fill, backfill ---- */

for (fld_ptr=1; fld_ptr <= fld_ct; fld_ptr++){
    find_field(scrn_no,fld_ptr);            /* set cursor for this field */
    sb = scrn_data + fld_ptr - 1;           /* point to field description */
    bfptr = sb -) item_value;               /* point to collection buff */
    len = s_ [scrn_no - 1].f_ [fld_ptr - 1].f_len;/* length */
    *(bfptr + len) = '\0';                  /* supply a null terminator */
    if (!sb -) fill_data)
        while (len--)
            *bfptr++ = ' ';                 /* fill with blanks */
    else if (sb -) ditto && sb -) dit_ptr)
        strcpy(bfptr, sb -) dit_ptr);       /* fill with ditto data */
    else while (len--) {
        if (!isprint(*bfptr))
            *bfptr = ' ';                   /* if trash inthe buffer */
        bfptr++;
    }
    backfill(scrn_no,fld_ptr,scrn_data);    /* fill the field with data */
}
fld_ptr = 1;
done = FALSE;

/* ---- collect data from the keyboard into the screen fields ---- */

while (!done)   {
    sb = scrn_data + fld_ptr - 1;
    bfptr = sb -) item_value;
    edit_mask = find_field(scrn_no,fld_ptr);
    if (sb -) protect)              /* ----- a protected field ------ */
        prev= ex = fld_ptr == 1 || fld_ptr == fld_ct ? '\r' : prev;
    else    {                       /* ----- get the data for this field --- */
        cursor(last_x, last_y);
        ex = get_data(sb -) item_type, edit_mask, bfptr);
```

Listing A-13 (continued)

```
        prev = ex != HELP && ex != DITTO ? ex : '\r';
        s_[scrn_no-1].f_[fld_ptr-1].din != !spaces(bfptr);
}
edit_funct = sb -) edits;
help_funct = sb -) helps;
if (ex == ESC)                       /* ---- if ESCAPE was typed ---- */
    break;
    edit_result = OK;                /* ---- pre-set ---- */
    if (!sb -) protect && ex != HELP && edit_funct)
        edit_result = (*edit_funct)(bfptr,ex);/* -- user edit -- */
    if (edit_result == OK)
        switch (ex) {                /* passed edit, how did it terminate? */
            case HELP:               /* help function key */
                if (help_funct) {
                    char1 = (*help_funct)();
                    if (*char1)
                        strcpy(bfptr,char1);

                }
                break;
            case DITTO:              /* ditto function key */
                if (sb -) dit_ptr)  {
                    strcpy(bfptr, sb -) dit_ptr);
                    cursor(last_x, last_y);
                    backfill(scrn_no,fld_ptr,scrn_data);
                }
            /* NOTE: ditto falls through to \r */
            case '\0':               /* out of last field on screen */
            case '\r':               /* enter/return */
                if (go_last && fld_ptr == fld_ct){
                    done = TRUE;
                    break;
                }
            /* NOTE: \r falls through to fwd */
            case '\t':               /* horizontal tab */
            case FWD:                /* -) */
                if (fld_ptr == fld_ct)
                    fld_ptr = 1;
                else
                    fld_ptr++;
                break;
            case '\b':               /* back space */
                if (fld_ptr == 1)
                    fld_ptr = fld_ct;
                else
                    fld_ptr--;
                break;
            case UP:                 /* cursor up key */

                f = fld_ptr;
                this_y = last_y;
```

Listing A-13 (continued)

```
            this_x = last_x;
            while (last_y == this_y && f > 1)
                find_field(scrn_no, --f);
            if (last_y == this_y)   {
                find_field(scrn_no, fld_ptr);
                break;
            }
            this_y = last_y;
            while (last_x > this_x
                    && this_y == last_y && f > 1)
                find_field(scrn_no, --f);
            if (this_y != last_y)
                f++;
            fld_ptr = f;
            break;
        case '\r':                  /* cursor down key */
            f = fld_ptr;
            this_y = last_y;
            this_x = last_x;
            while (last_y == this_y
                    && f < s_ [scrn_no - 1].no_flds)
                find_field(scrn_no, ++f);
            if (f == s_ [scrn_no - 1].no_flds)
                prev = '\r';
            if (last_y == this_y)   {
                find_field(scrn_no, fld_ptr);
                break;
            }
            this_y = last_y;
            while (last_x < this_x && this_y == last_y
                    && f < s_ [scrn_no - 1].no_flds)
                find_field(scrn_no, ++f);
            if (this_y != last_y)
                f--;
            fld_ptr = f;
            break;
        case GO:                    /* GO function key */

/* these cases are the function keys. F1, F2 and F3 are already
   processed as GO, HELP and DITTO.  */

        case F4:
        case F5:
        case F6:
        case F7:
        case F8:
        case F9:
        case F10:
            done = TRUE;
            break;
```

Listing A-13 (continued)

```
            default:
                break;
        }
}

/* ----- all the fields are in, copy ditto fields to ditto hold areas --- */
for (fld_ptr = 1; fld_ptr <= fld_ct; fld_ptr++){
    sb = scrn_data + fld_ptr - 1;
    if (sb -> dit_ptr)
        strcpy(sb -> dit_ptr, sb -> item_value);
}

    return (ex);        /* return the key that terminated entry of this data */
}




/* ---------For callers to rebuild the screen after they have used it
                    (e.g. for HELP) -------------- */

VOID disp_scrn(scrn_no, scrn_data)
int scrn_no;
struct scrn_buf *scrn_data;
{
    register int fld_p;

    display_crt(scrn_no);
    for (fld_p = 1; fld_p <= s_ [scrn_no - 1].no_flds; fld_p++)
        backfill(scrn_no, fld_p, scrn_data);
}




/* -------- A utility for callers of the package. It gets data in for a single
    field on the screen --------------- */

char get_item(sc, crt, fld)
struct scrn_buf *sc;       /* points to user's screen definition */
int crt;                   /* screen number in file  */
int fld;                   /* field number on screen */
{
    register char *m;
    char get_data(), c;

    sc += (fld - 1);
    m = find_field(crt, fld);
    cursor(last_x, last_y);
    c = get_data(sc -> item_type, m, sc -> item_value);
    s_[crt-1].f_[fld-1].din != !spaces(sc->item_value);
    return c;
}
```

Listing A-13 (continued)

```
/* ------- fill an item from the screen's data onto the screen. ------- */

VOID backfill(crt,item,screen_data)
struct scrn_buf *screen_data;
int item,crt;
{
    int i;
    register char *str, *mask;
    char *find_field();
    struct scrn_buf *sptr;

    sptr = screen_data + item - 1;
    str = sptr -) item_value;
    if (spaces(str) && s_ [crt - 1].f_ [item - 1].din == FALSE)
        return;
    s_ [crt - 1].f_ [item - 1].din = !spaces(str);
    mask = find_field(crt,item);    /* -) field mask of underlines */
    cursor (last_x, last_y);
    if (sptr -) protect)
        high_intensity(FALSE);           /* protected fields are 1/2 intensity */
    else
        high_intensity(TRUE);            /* unprotected fields are full intensity */
    underline(TRUE);                 /* data fields are always underlined */
    disp_fld(str,mask);         /* display the field */
    underline(FALSE);                /* turn off underline */
    high_intensity(FALSE);           /* 1/2 intensity */
}


/* -------------- Standard error message function -------- */

VOID err_msg(s)
char *s;
{
    save_gr();
    put_byte(BELL);            /* ding! */
    high_intensity(TRUE);      /* errors are bright */
    notice(s);                 /* post the error */
    rstr_gr();
}


/* --------- clear the message/notice line ------------ */

VOID clrmsg()
{
    register int i;

    if (msg_up) {    /* only if one is displayed */
        save_gr();
```

Listing A-13 (continued)

```
        high_intensity(FALSE);
        underline(FALSE);
        cursor(0,0);
        for (i = 0; i < 50; i++)
            put_byte(' ');
        msg_up = FALSE;
        cursor(last_x, last_y);
        rstr_gr();
    }
}


/* ---------- Standard notice function ----------------- */

VOID notice(s)
char *s;
{
    save_gr();
    underline(FALSE);              /* notices are not underlined */
    clrmsg();                /* clear any old message */
    cursor(0,0);
    while (*s) {
        if (!isprint(*s))    /* in case of trash */
            *s = '^';
        put_byte(*s++);
    }
    rstr_gr();
    cursor(last_x, last_y);
    msg_up = TRUE;
}


/* ----------- Display the crt template specified by crt ----------- */
VOID display_crt(crt)
int crt;
{
    register char *cptr;
    char c;
    int x = 0, filling = FALSE;

    clr_scrn();
    cptr = s_ [crt-1].s_mptr;              /* -> the screen template */
    while ((c = *cptr++) != SCRNID)        /* until another screen or end */
        if (c)    {
            if (c == FLDFILL)   {          /* field? */
                c = ' ';                   /* displayed as space */
                if (!filling)    {
                    filling = TRUE;
                    high_intensity(TRUE);      /* fields are bright */
                    underline(TRUE);           /* and underlined */
                }
```

Listing A-13 (continued)

```
            }
            else if (filling)    {              /* not a field */
                filling = FALSE;
                high_intensity(FALSE);          /* dim */
                underline(FALSE);               /* and plain */
            }
            if (c != '\t')    {
                x++;                            /* everything but tabs */
                put_byte(c);
            }
            else        {                       /* tabs */
                put_byte(' ');
                while (++x % HT)
                    put_byte(' ');
            }

            if (c == '\n' || c == '\r')
                x = 0;                          /* set x for tab logic */
        }
    insert_line();                              /* post insert toggle */
}


/* --------- Put cursor at 1st position of field f. ------------ */

char *find_field(crt,f)
int crt, f;
{
    last_x = s_ [crt - 1].f_ [f - 1].f_x;
    last_y = s_ [crt - 1].f_ [f - 1].f_y;
    return s_ [crt - 1].f_ [f - 1].f_mptr;
}


/* ------- Get data item from k/b. use data type and mask to edit & ctl length.
   Return terminating byte (/n, /t, esc) ------------- */

char get_data(type,msk,bf)
char type, *msk, *bf;
{
    char *end_buf, c, *b;
    register char *mask, *buff;
    int depart, digits, chok, x, i;

    buff = bf;
    mask = msk;
    depart = FALSE;
    digits = FALSE;
    high_intensity(TRUE);
    underline(TRUE);
```

Listing A-13 (continued)

```
if (type == 'C')    {                        /* currency? */
    x = last_x;
    while (*mask != '.')    {                 /* look for . */
        if (!(punct(*mask)))
            buff++;
        mask++;
        last_x++;
    }
    last_x--;                                 /* one before the . */
    cursor(last_x, last_y);            /* cursor at units of whole dollars */
    buff--;

    /* ---- wait for the . or a key to get us out of the number ---- */

    while ((c = get_byte()) != '\r' && c != ESC && c != '.'
        && c != '\t' && c != UP && c != '\n' && c != FWD
            && c != '\b' && c != GO)    {
        i = c == ' ' ? TRUE : isnumr(c);      /* allow ' ' or digit */
        if (i)    {
            movmem(bf + 1, bf, buff - bf); /* shift the number, calculator style *
            *buff = c;                        /* put in latest digit */
            cursor(x, last_y);
            disp_fld(bf, msk);                /* display number */
            cursor(last_x, last_y);           /* position cursor at units digit */
        }

    }
    b = bf;
    while (b (= buff && (*b == ' ' || *b == '0'))
        *b++ = ' ';                           /* space fill leading zeros */
    cursor(x, last_y);
    disp_fld(bf, msk);
    cursor(last_x, last_y);
    if (c == '\r'  || c == GO || c == '\b' || c == UP || c == '\n' || c == ESC){
        high_intensity(FALSE);
        underline(FALSE);
        return (c);      /* if departing this currency field while in dollars */
    }
    mask++;

    buff++;
    bf = buff;
    msk = mask;
    put_byte(FWD);        /* get past the decimal point on the display */
    put_byte(FWD);
    last_x += 2;

    /* ---- the decimal part is treated further down as a numeric entry ----- */

}
/* --------- read in a data field from the keyboard ---------- */
```

Listing A-13 (continued)

```
while (TRUE)    {              /* until a keystroke terminates entry */
    c = get_byte();            /* get a character of data entry */
    clrmsg();
    switch (c) {               /* what was it? */
        case '\r':
        case '\n':
        case '\t':
        case DITTO:
        case ESC:
        case GO:
        case HELP:
        case F4:
        case F5:
        case F6:
        case F7:
        case F8:
        case F9:
        case F10:
        case UP:

            depart = TRUE;     /* all of the above terminate entry */
            break;
        case '\b':             /* back space */
            if (buff == bf) {  /* if at beginning of field, terminate */
                depart = TRUE;
                break;
            }
        case RUBOUT:           /* rubout or backspace */
            if (buff == bf)
                break;
            --buff;            /* decrement the pointers */
            --mask;
            if (punct(*mask))    {   /* go backwards around the punctuation */
                put_byte('\b');
                last_x--;
                --mask;
            }
            put_byte('\b');        /* backspace */
            last_x--;
            if (c != RUBOUT)    {
                /* -- keep track of digits entered for numerics -- */
                if (type == 'N' && (*(buff-1) == ' ' || buff == bf))
                    digits = FALSE;
                break;
            }
        case DELETE:               /* backspace, rubout, delete */

            for (b=buff; *b != '\0'; b++)
                *b = *(b+1);
            *--b = ' ';            /* shift data one space to left */
            disp_fld(buff,mask);
```

Listing A-13 (continued)

```
        if (type == 'N' && buff > bf && *(buff-1) != ' ')
            digits = TRUE;       /* keep track of digits */
        break;
    case FWD:                    /* cursor forward */
        put_byte(FWD);
        last_x++;
        mask++;
        if (punct(*mask))    {   /* bypass punctuation */
            put_byte(FWD);
            last_x++;
            mask++;
        }
        buff++;
        break;
    case INSERT:                 /* INSERT toggle function key */
        inserting ^= TRUE;       /* flip the toggle */
        insert_line();           /* display the current value */
        break;
    default:                     /* all other keystrokes */
        switch (type)   {        /* what to do is based on data type */
            case 'A':            /* alphanumeric */
                if (!(chok = isprint(c)))/* must be printable key */
                    err_msg("Invalid keystroke");
                break;
            case 'C':            /* currency (decimal part) */
            case 'N':            /* numeric space filled */
                if (chok = (!digits && c == ' '))
                    break;       /* must be digit or space */
            case 'D':            /* date */
            case 'Z':            /* numeric, zero fill */
                chok = isnumr(c);   /* must be digit */
                break;
            default:
                break;
        }
        if (chok)   {            /* chok = TRUE if stroke was ok */
            if (inserting) {           /* insert mode? */
                for (b=buff; *b != '\0'; b++)/* scan to end of string */
                    ;
                b--;
                while (b != buff)   {   /* shift 1 char to right */
                    *b = *(b - 1);
                    b--;
                }
                disp_fld(buff,mask);
            }
            if (type == 'N' && c != ' ')
                digits = TRUE;
            *buff++ = c;                 /* put in new char */
            put_byte(c);                 /* echo it */
```

Listing A-13 (continued)

```
        last_x++;
        mask++;

                if (punct(*mask))    {          /* bypass punctuation */
                    put_byte(FWD);
                    last_x++;
                    mask++;
                }
            }
    }
    if (*mask == '\0')                          /* if at end of field */
        depart = TRUE;
    if (depart) {                               /* if this field is done */
        if (type != 'D' || c == ESC)            /* non-date needs no more edits, */
            break;                              /* nor does escqpe */
        if (edit_date(bf) == OK)                /* edit the date entry */
            break;
        depart = FALSE;                         /* date failed, don't let it out */
        while (buff > bf)    {                   /* back up to first char of date  */
            --buff;
            --mask;

                if (punct(*mask))    {
                    put_byte('\b');
                    last_x--;
                    --mask;
                }
                put_byte('\b');
                last_x--;
        }
    }
}

if (c != ESC && c != HELP)   {
    if (*mask == '\0' && c != FWD)
        c = '\0';
    if (type == 'N' || type == 'Z' || type == 'C'){
        if (type =='N')
            r_just(bf);             /* right just, space fill N fields */
        else if (type == 'Z')
            z_just(bf);             /* right just, zero fill Z fields */
        else
            zl_just(bf);            /* left just, zero fill C decimal parts */
        while (mask-- != msk)
            put_byte('\b');
        disp_fld(bf,msk);
    }
}
high_intensity(FALSE);
underline(FALSE);
return (c);
}
```

Listing A-13 (continued)

```
/* ----- edit a character for numerics.  post error message if not ---- */

int isnumr(c)
char c;
{
    int r;

    if (!(r = isdigit(c)))
        err_msg("Numbers only");
    return r;
}




/* ------- Right justify, space fill a numeric field -------- */

VOID r_just(s)
char *s;

{
    register int len;

    len = strlen(s);
    while (*s == ' ' || *s == '0' && len)   {
        len--;
        *s++ = ' ';
    }
    if (len)   {
        while (*(s + (len - 1)) == ' ') {
            movmem(s, s + 1, len - 1);
            *s = ' ';
        }
    }
}




/* ---------- Right justify, zero fill a numeric field --------------- */

VOID z_just(s)
char *s;
{
    register int len;

    if (spaces(s))
        return;

    len = strlen(s);
    while (*(s + len - 1) == ' ')   {
```

Listing A-13 (continued)

```
        movmem(s, s + 1, len-1);
        *s = '0';
    }
}


/* ------------ zero fill on the right ---------------------- */

VOID zl_just(s)
char *s;
{
    while (*s)  {
        if (*s == ' ')
            *s = '0';
        s++;
    }
}


/* ---------- test a string for spaces. return TRUE if all spaces -------- */

int spaces(c)
char *c;
{
    while (*c == ' ')
        c++;
    if (!*c)
        return TRUE;            /* if null string terminator */
    return FALSE;
}


/* ------------- edit a date ---------------- */

int edit_date(date)
char *date;
{
    static int days [12] = { 31,28,31,30,31,30,31,31,30,31,30,31 };
    int mo, da, yr;
    static char mm [] = "00", dd [] = "00";

    if (spaces(date))
        return OK;                  /* it's ok to leave a date blank */
    yr = atoi(date+4);
    days [1] = yr % 4 ? 28 : 29;    /* leap year test. good until 2100  */
                                    /* with only 2 digits of year,      */
                                    /* 00 is assumed to be 2000.        */
    sprintf(mm, "%02.2s", date);
    sprintf(dd, "%02.2s", date + 2);
```

Listing A-13 (continued)

```
    mo = atoi(mm);
    if (!mo || mo > 12) {              /* can't be more than December */
        err_msg("Invalid month");
        return ERROR;
    }
    da = atoi(dd);
    if (da && da <= days [mo - 1])    /* day can't be more than month hath */
        return OK;
    err_msg("Invalid day");
    return ERROR;
}



/* ---------- Display a field value based upon its display mask -------- */
VOID disp_fld(b,mask)
char *b, *mask;
{
    register char *m;

    m = mask;
    while (*m)  {
        if (punct(*m))  {             /* bypass punctuation in the mask */
            m++;
            put_byte(FWD);
            if (!*m)                  /* in cases the punctuation is at the end */
                break;
        }
        if (!isprint(*b))             /* in case of trash in the data */
            put_byte('^');
        else
            put_byte(*b);
        b++;
        m++;
    }
    while ((m--) - mask)
        put_byte('\b');               /* put the cursor back at the start */
}



/* ---------- Post (INSERT) token ------------------ */
VOID insert_line()
{
    save_gr();
    underline(FALSE);
    cursor(55,0);
    printf(inserting ? "(INSERT)" : "        ");
    cursor(last_x,last_y);
```

Listing A-13 (continued)

```
    rstr_gr();
}



/* ----------- Return TRUE if c is a punctuation character.
    Otherwise return FALSE. -------------------  */

int punct(c)
char c;
{
/* ---- some applications have different requirements for this table ---- */
    return (c == '/' || c == '.' || c == '-' || c == ':'
                || c == '(' || c == ')' || c == ',');
}
```

```
/* ------------------ sort.h ------------------------- */

#define NOFLDS 5                 /* maximum number of fields to sort */

struct s_prm {                   /* sort parameters  */
    int rc_len;                  /* record length    */
    char sort_drive;             /* disk drive for work file*/
                                 /* 1, 2, ...,  = A, B, ...,*/
                                 /* NULL = current logged on drive*/

    struct {
        int f_pos;               /* 1st position of field (rel 1)*/
        int f_len;               /* length of field  */
        char az;                 /* A = ascending; Z = descending*/
    } s_fld [NOFLDS];            /* one per field    */
};


int init_sort();                 /*    Initialize the sort*/
VOID sort();                     /*    Pass records to Sort*/
char *sort_op();                 /*    Retrieve sorted records*/
VOID sort_stats();               /*    Display sort statistics*/
VOID qsort();                    /*    Quicksort algorithm*/
```

Listing A-14.

```
/* ---------------------- sort.c ---------------------------- */

#include <stdio.h>
#include "toolset.h"
#if COMPILER != CWARE
#if COMPILER != MWC
#include <fcntl.h>
#endif
#endif
#include "sort.h"

#define MOSTMEM 50000    /* the most memory to allocate for sort buffer */
#define LEASTMEM 10240   /* the least memory acceptable for sort buffer */

struct bp    {           /* one of these for each sequence in merge buffer */
    char *rc;            /* -) record in merge buffer */
    int rbuf;            /* number of records left in buffer this sequence */
    int rdsk;            /* number of records left on disk this sequence */
    };
struct s_prm *sp;        /* structure of sort parameters */
int totrcd;              /* total records sorted */
int no_seq;              /* counts sequences */
int no_seq1;
unsigned h;              /* amount of available buffer space */
int nrcds;               /* constant number of records in sort buffer */
int nrcds1;
char *bf, *bf1;          /* points to sort buffer */
int inbf;                /* variable records in sort buffer */
char **sptr;             /* points to array of buffer pointers */
char *init_sptr;         /* constant pointer to appropriated buffer */
int n;                   /* number of rcds/sequence in merge buffer */
int comp();              /* comparison function */
int fd, f2;              /* sort work file fds */
char fdname [15];        /* sort work name */
char f2name [15];        /* sort work name */
VOID prep_merge(), merge(), dumpbuff();
char *malloc();


/* --------Function to initialize sort global variables---------- */

int init_sort(prms)
struct s_prm *prms;
{
    char *appr_mem();

    sp = prms;
    if (bf = appr_mem(&h)) {
        nrcds1 = nrcds = h / (sp->rc_len + sizeof(char *));
        init_sptr = bf;
```

Listing A-15.

Listing A-15 (continued)

```c
        sptr = (char **) bf;
        bf += nrcds * sizeof(char *);
        fd = f2 = totrcd = no_seq = inbf = 0;
        return OK;
    }
    else
        return ERROR;
}



/* --------- Function to accept records to sort ---------------- */
VOID sort(s_rcd)
char *s_rcd;
{
    if (inbf == nrcds) {                  /* if the sort buffer is full */
        qsort(init_sptr, inbf, comp);     /* sort the buffer */
        if (s_rcd) {                      /* if there are more records to sort */
            dumpbuff();                   /* dump the buffer to a sort work file */
            no_seq++;                     /* count the sorted sequences */
        }
    }
    if (s_rcd) {                          /* if this is a record to sort */
        totrcd++;                         /* count records */
        *sptr = bf + inbf * sp->rc_len;   /* put a rcd addr in the pointer array */
        inbf++;                           /* count rcds in the buffer */
        movmem(s_rcd, *sptr, sp->rc_len); /* move the rcd to the buffer */
        sptr++;                           /* point to next array entry */
    }
    else    {                             /* null pointer means no more rcds */
        if (inbf)    {                    /* any records in the buffer? */
            qsort(init_sptr, inbf, comp); /* sort them */
            if (no_seq)                   /* if this isn't the only sequence */
                dumpbuff();               /* dump the buffer to a work file */
            no_seq++;                     /* count the sequence */
        }
        no_seq1 = no_seq;
        if (no_seq > 1)                   /* if there is more than 1 sequence */
            prep_merge();                 /* prepare for the merge of sequences */
    }
}


/* -------------------- Prepare for the merge -------------------- */
VOID prep_merge()
{
    register int i;
    int hd;
    register struct bp *rr;
    unsigned n_bfsz;
```

Listing A-15 (continued)

```
    n_bfsz = h - no_seq * sizeof(struct bp);    /* merge buff size */
    n = n_bfsz / no_seq / sp->rc_len;            /* # rcds/seq in mrg buff */
    if (n < 2) {
        f2 = wopen(f2name, 2);                   /* open a sort work file */
        while (n < 2)    {
            merge();                             /* binary merge */
            hd = fd;                             /* swap fds */
            fd = f2;
            f2 = hd;
            nrcds *= 2;
            no_seq = (no_seq + 1) / 2;           /* adjust number of sequences */
            n_bfsz = h - no_seq * sizeof(struct bp);
            n = n_bfsz / no_seq / sp->rc_len;
        }
    }
    bf1 = init_sptr;
    rr = (struct bp *) init_sptr;
    bf1 += no_seq * sizeof(struct bp);
    bf = bf1;

    /* --------- fill the merge buffer with records from all sequences ---*/

    for (i = 0; i < no_seq; i++)    {
        lseek(fd, (long) i * ((long) nrcds * sp->rc_len), 0);
        read(fd, bf1, n * sp->rc_len);          /* read them all at once */
        rr->rc = bf1;
        if (i == no_seq-1) {        /* last seq has fewer rcds than the rest */
            if (totrcd % nrcds > n)    {
                rr->rbuf = n;
                rr->rdsk = (totrcd % nrcds) - n;
            }
            else    {
                rr->rbuf = totrcd % nrcds;
                rr->rdsk = 0;
            }
        }
        else    {
            rr->rbuf = n;
            rr->rdsk = nrcds - n;
        }
        rr++;
        bf1 += n * sp->rc_len;
    }
}

/* ------------------- Merge the work file down -------------------
This is a binary merge of records from of sequences in fd into f2.  */

VOID merge()
{
```

Listing A-15 (continued)

```
        register int i;
        int needy, needx;       /* logical switches. true = need a rcd from (x/y) */
        int xcnt, ycnt;         /* # rcds left each sequence */
        int x, y;               /* sequence counters */
        long adx, ady;          /* sequence record disk addresses */


/* --- the two sets of sequences are thought of as x and y ----- */
    lseek(f2, 0L, 0);                       /* --- beginning of output file --- */
    for (i = 0; i < no_seq; i += 2)     {
        x = y = i;
        y++;
        ycnt = y == no_seq ? 0 : y == no_seq - 1 ? totrcd % nrcds : nrcds;
        xcnt = y == no_seq ? totrcd % nrcds : nrcds;
        adx = (long) x * (long) nrcds * sp->rc_len;
        ady = adx + (long) nrcds * sp ->rc_len;
        needy = needx = TRUE;
        while (xcnt || ycnt)    {
            if (needx && xcnt) {    /* need a rcd from x? */
                lseek(fd, adx, 0);
                adx += (long) sp->rc_len;
                read(fd, init_sptr, sp->rc_len);
                needx = FALSE;
            }
            if (needy && ycnt) {    /* need a rcd from y? */
                lseek(fd, ady, 0);
                ady += sp->rc_len;
                read(fd, init_sptr + sp->rc_len, sp->rc_len);
                needy = FALSE;
            }
            if (xcnt || ycnt)   {    /* if anything is left */
                /* ---- compare data between the two sequences --- */
                if (!ycnt ||
                    (xcnt && (comp(init_sptr, init_sptr + sp->rc_len)) < 0)){
                            /* -- data from x is lower -- */
                    write(f2, init_sptr, sp->rc_len);
                    --xcnt;
                    needx = TRUE;


                }
                else if (ycnt) { /*  data from y is lower */
                    write(f2, init_sptr + sp->rc_len, sp->rc_len);
                    --ycnt;
                    needy = TRUE;
                }
            }
        }
    }
}
```

Listing A-15 (continued)

```
/* --------------- Dump the sort buffer to the work file ----------- */

VOID dumpbuff()
{
    register int i;

    if (!fd)                                /* 1st time in */
        fd = wopen(fdname, 1);
    sptr = (char **) init_sptr;
    for (i = 0; i < inbf; i++)  {
        write(fd, *(sptr + i), sp->rc_len); /* the pointers were sorted */
        *(sptr + i) = 0;
    }
    inbf = 0;
}




/* --------------- Open a sort work file --------------------- */

int wopen(name, n)
char *name;
int n;
{

        int fd;

        *name = '\0';
        if (sp->sort_drive) {
            strcpy(name, "A:");
            *name += (sp->sort_drive - 1);
        }
        strcat(name, "sortwork.000");
        name [strlen(name) - 1] += n;
        fd = creat(name, CMODE);
        close(fd);
        return open(name, O_RDWR);
}




/* -------------- Function to get sorted records --------------------
This is called to get sorted records after the sort is done.  It
returns pointers to each sorted record.  Each call to it returns one
record.  When there are no more records, it returns NULL. ------ */

char *sort_op()
{
```

Listing A-15 (continued)

```c
int j = 0;
int nrd, i, k, l, m;
register struct bp *rr;
static int r1 = 0;
register char *rtn;
long ad, tr;

sptr = (char **) init_sptr;
if (no_seq < 2) {    /* with only 1 sequence, no merge has been done */
    if (r1 == totrcd)
        return NULL;
    return *(sptr + r1++);
}
rr = (struct bp *) init_sptr;
for (i = 0; i < no_seq; i++)
    j |= (rr + i)->rbuf | (rr + i)->rdsk; /* any rcds left? */

/* -------- j will be true if any sequence still has records ------ */

if (!j)    {
    close(fd);              /* none left */
    unlink(fdname);
    if (f2) {
        close(f2);
        unlink(f2name);
    }
    free(init_sptr);
    return NULL;
}
k = 0;

/* --- find the sequence in the merge buffer with the lowest record --- */

for (i = 0; i < no_seq; i++)    {
    m = ((comp ((rr + k)->rc, (rr + i)->rc) < 0) ? k : i);
    k = m;
}


/* --- k is an integer sequence number that offsets to the
    sequence with the lowest record ---- */

(rr + k)->rbuf--;                        /* decrement the rcd counter */
rtn = (rr + k)->rc;                      /* set the return pointer */
(rr + k)->rc += sp->rc_len;
if ((rr + k)->rbuf == 0)    {            /* -- if the sequence got empty, */
    rtn = bf + k * n * sp->rc_len;       /* get some more if there are any --- */
    movmem((rr + k)->rc - sp->rc_len, rtn, sp->rc_len);

    (rr + k)->rc = rtn + sp->rc_len;
    if ((rr + k)->rdsk != 0)    {
```

Listing A-15 (continued)

```
            l = ((n - 1) ( (rr + k)-)rdsk) ? n - 1 : (rr + k)-)rdsk;
            nrd = k == no_seq - 1 ? totrcd % nrcds : nrcds;
            tr = (long) ((k * nrcds + (nrd - (rr + k)-)rdsk)));
            ad = tr * sp-)rc_len;
            lseek(fd, ad, 0);
            read(fd, rtn + sp-)rc_len, l * sp-)rc_len);
            (rr + k)-)rbuf = l;
            (rr + k)-)rdsk -= l;
        }
        else
            setmem((rr + k)-)rc, sp-)rc_len, 127);
    }
    return (rtn);
}


/* ---------- Function to display sort statistics ---------------- */

VOID sort_stats()
{
    printf("\n\n\nRecord Length = %d",sp-)rc_len);
    printf("\n%d records sorted",totrcd);
    printf("\n%d sequences",no_seq1);
    printf("\n%u characters of sort buffer", h);
    printf("\n%d records per buffer\n\n",nrcds1);
}




/* ------- appropriate what memory is available --------------- */

char *appr_mem(h)
unsigned *h;
{
    char *buff = 0;

    *h = (unsigned) MOSTMEM + 1024;
    while (buff == 0 && *h ) LEASTMEM)  {
        *h -= 1024;
        buff = malloc(*h);
    }
    return buff;
}




/* ----------- compare function for sorting, merging ------------- */

int comp(a, b)
char *a, *b;
{
    register int i, J;
    int k, r;
```

Listing A-15 (continued)

```
    if (*a == 127 || *b == 127)
        return *a - *b;
    for (i = 0; i < NOFLDS; i++)
        for (j = 0; j < sp->s_fld[i].f_len; j++)
            if (k = (int) *(a + sp->s_fld[i].f_pos - 1 + j) -
                    (int) *(b + sp->s_fld[i].f_pos - 1 + j))
                return (toupper(sp->s_fld[i].az) == 'Z') ? -k : k;
    return 0;
}


/* ----------------- qsort algorithm ----------------------------- */
VOID qsort(p, n, comp)
register char *p [];       /* points to an array of character pointers */
int n;                     /* with n entries */
int (*comp)();             /* the compare function provided by the caller */
{
    int i = 0, j;
    register char *k;
    register char *l;
    if (n < 2)
        return;
    j = n;
    k = p [j/2];           /* approximate median key */
    p [j/2] = p [0];
    p [0] = k;
    while (1)    {
        while ((*comp)(p [++i], k) < 0 && i < j - 1)
            ;
        while ((*comp)(p [--j], k) > 0)
            ;
        if (i < j) {
            l = p [j];
            p [j] = p [i];
            p [i] = l;
        }
        else
            break;
    }
    p [0] = p [j];
    p [j] = k;
    qsort(p, j, comp);
    qsort(p+j+1, n-j-1, comp);
}
```

```
/* ------------------------ btree.h ------------------- */

int init_b();          /*    Initializes a B-tree index      */
int close_b();         /*    Closes a B-tree index file      */
int find_key();        /*    Searches a B-tree for a key     */
int insert_key();      /*    Inserts a key into a B-tree     */
int delete_key();      /*    Deletes a key from a B-tree     */
ADDR get_next();       /*    Gets address of the next key    */
ADDR get_prev();       /*    Gets address of the previous key */
ADDR find_first();     /*    Gets address of first key       */
ADDR find_last();      /*    Gets address of last key        */

#define MXKEY 25        /* maximum key length  */
#define MAXNDX 5        /* maximum number of trees open  */

struct b_node   {
    int isnode;     /* 0 if leaf, 1 if node  */
    union   {
        ADDR prnt;  /* node # of parent of this node/leaf */
        ADDR dlptr; /* linked list pointer for deleted nodes */
    } bu;
    ADDR l_bro;     /* node # of left sibling node  */
    ADDR r_bro;     /* node # of right sibling node  */
    int nkeys;      /* number of keys in this node  */
    ADDR faddr;     /* node # of keys < 1st key this node  */
    char kdat [1];  /* 1st byte of 1st key  */
};

struct b_hdr    {
    ADDR root;      /* node # of root of this tree */
    int klen;       /* length of key in this tree  */
    int m;          /* number of keys allowed in a node  */
    ADDR nxt_free;  /* node # of next free node */
    ADDR nxt_avail; /* node # of next available node  */
    int in_use;     /* TRUE when b tree is in use  */
    ADDR lmost;     /* node # of left most node among leaves */
    ADDR rmost;     /* right most node */
};
```

Listing A-16.

```
/* ------------------------- btree.c ------------------------- */

#include (stdio.h)
#include "toolset.h"
#if COMPILER != CWARE
#if COMPILER != MWC
#include (fcntl.h)
#endif
#endif
#include "btree.h"
#include "cache.h"

int b_fd;                   /* file descriptor of b-tree file  */

int fds     [MAXNDX];       /* fds of each index in use  */
ADDR b_nbr [MAXNDX];        /* node number of current key */
int k_ptr  [MAXNDX];        /* key number of current key in node  */
VOID even_dist();
VOID combine_nodes();
char *malloc();

/* -------- User call to initiate b tree index processing ---------- */

int init_b(ndx_name, len)
char *ndx_name;     /* name of b tree index file  */
int len;            /* length of key in index  */
{
    register struct b_hdr *hp;
    int i;
    for (i = 0; i ( MAXNDX; i++)
        if (fds [i] == 0)
            break;
    if (i == MAXNDX)
        return ERROR;
    init_cache();
    if ((b_fd = open(ndx_name, 2)) == ERROR)    {
        printf("\nBuilding new index file %s\n", ndx_name);
        b_fd = build_b(ndx_name, len);
    }
    hp = (struct b_hdr *) get_node(b_fd, (ADDR) 1);
    if (hp-)in_use) {
        printf("\nIndex file %s", ndx_name);
        fatal(3);
    }
    hp-)in_use = TRUE;
    release_node(b_fd, (ADDR) 1, 1);
    flush_cache(b_fd);
    fds [i] = b_fd;
    b_nbr [i] = 0;
    return i;
}
```

Listing A-17.

Listing A-17 (continued)

```
/* ----------- User call to complete b tree index processing ------------- */

int close_b(tree)
int tree;
{
    register struct b_hdr *hp;

    if (tree )= MAXNDX || fds [tree] == 0)
        return ERROR;
    b_fd = fds [tree];
    hp = (struct b_hdr *) get_node(b_fd, (ADDR) 1);
    hp->in_use = FALSE;
    release_node(b_fd, (ADDR) 1, 1);
    flush_cache(b_fd);
    close(b_fd);
    fds [tree] = 0;
    return OK;
}



/* --------Build a new b-tree disk file.   Return the fd ------------------ */

int build_b(name, len)
char *name;        /* name of the file */
int len;           /* length of a key in the tree */
{
    struct b_hdr *bh;
    int fd;

    if ((bh = (struct b_hdr *) malloc(NODELEN)) == 0)
        fatal(9);
    setmem(bh, NODELEN, '\0');
    bh->klen = len;
    bh->m = (NODELEN - (sizeof(struct b_node) - 1)) /
                        (len + sizeof(ADDR));
    bh->nxt_avail = 2;
    fd = creat(name, CMODE);
    close(fd);
    fd = open(name, O_RDWR);
    write(fd, bh, NODELEN);
    free(bh);
    return fd;
}



/* --------------- Find the 1st occurrence of key k in the b-tree.
    Return TRUE if key is found.
    Return FALSE if key not found.
    Return the file address of = or higher node in ad ------------------ */
```

```
int find_key(tree, k, ad)
int tree;
char *k;
ADDR *ad;
{
    struct b_node *pp;
    register struct b_hdr *hp;
    int fnd, i;
    ADDR ans, t, q;
    ADDR find_leaf();
    char *a;


    if (tree )= MAXNDX || fds [tree] == 0)
        return FALSE;
    b_fd = fds [tree];
    hp = (struct b_hdr *) get_node(b_fd, (ADDR) 1);
    t = hp->root;
    if (t) {
        pp = (struct b_node *) get_node(b_fd, t);
        fnd = search_tree(&t, &pp, hp, k, &a);
        ans = find_leaf(&t, &pp, hp, &a, &i);
        q = t;
        if (i == pp->nkeys + 1) {
            i = 0;
            t = pp->r_bro;
            if (t) {
                release_node(b_fd, q, 0);
                pp = (struct b_node *) get_node(b_fd, t);
                ans = pp->faddr;
                q = t;
            }
            else
                ans = 0;
        }
        b_nbr [tree] = t;
        k_ptr [tree] = i;
        *ad = ans;
        release_node(b_fd, q, 0);


    }
    else {
        *ad = 0;
        fnd = FALSE;
    }
    release_node(b_fd, (ADDR) 1, 0);
    return fnd;
}
```

Listing A-17 (continued)

```
/* ---- Search tree t for node k. Return TRUE or FALSE depending upon search.
   Set pp -) the node in which search stopped.   Set a -) the key )= k. --- */
static int search_tree(t, pp, hp, k, a)
ADDR *t;
struct b_node **pp;
struct b_hdr *hp;
char *k, **a;
{
    int nl;
    register ADDR *a_ptr;
    ADDR p, q, next_key(), prev_key();

    p = *t;
    q = 0;
    do {
        if (find_node(k, *pp, hp, a))   {
            while (!keycmp(*a, k, hp-)klen))
                if (!prev_key(&p, pp, hp, a))
                    break;
            if (keycmp(*a, k, hp-)klen))
                next_key(&p, pp, hp, a);
            *t = p;
            return TRUE;
        }
        q = p;
        a_ptr = (ADDR *) (*a - sizeof(ADDR));
        p = *a_ptr;
        nl = (*pp)-)isnode;
        if (nl)      {
            release_node(b_fd, q, 0);
            *pp = (struct b_node *) get_node(b_fd, p);
        }
    }      while (nl);
    *t = q;
    return FALSE;
}

/* ---- Find key k in node -)pp.  Rtn TRUE/FALSE.  Rtn addr of key in a. ---- */

static int find_node(k, pp, hp, a)
char *k, **a;
struct b_node *pp;
struct b_hdr *hp;
{
    register int i;
    int cm;

    *a = pp-)kdat;
    for (i = 0; i ( pp-)nkeys; i++) {
        cm = keycmp(k, *a, hp-)klen);
```

```
            if (!cm) return TRUE;
            if (cm < 0) return FALSE;
            *a += hp->klen + sizeof(ADDR);
        }
        return FALSE;
}


/* ------------- Compare two keys. Return the result ----------- */

static int keycmp(a, b, len)
char *a, *b;
int len;
{
    int cm;

    while (len--)
        if (cm = (int) *a++ - (int) *b++)
            break;
    return cm;
}


/* ------ Get the file address for the key pointed at by the pointers ---- */

static ADDR get_addr(t, pp, hp, a)
ADDR t;
struct b_node **pp;
struct b_hdr *hp;
char *a;
{
    ADDR cn, ti;
    ADDR find_leaf();
    int i;

    ti = t;
    cn = find_leaf(&ti, pp, hp, &a, &i);
    release_node(b_fd, ti, 0);
    *pp = (struct b_node *) get_node(b_fd, t);
    return cn;
}


/* ----- Find the leaf starting at the key position -) by a. Return the record
   address pointed to for the key. --------------------------- */

static ADDR find_leaf(t, pp, hp, a, p)
int *p;
ADDR *t;
struct b_node **pp;
struct b_hdr *hp;
char **a;
{
```

Listing A-17 (continued)

```
    ADDR ti, *b, *i;

    b = (ADDR *) (*a + hp-)klen);
    if (!(*pp)-)isnode) {              /* already at a leaf? */
        *p = (*a - (*pp)-)kdat) /
            (hp-)klen + sizeof(ADDR)) + 1;
        return *b;
    }
    *p = 0;
    i = b;
    release_node(b_fd, *t, 0);
    *t = *i;
    *pp = (struct b_node *) get_node(b_fd, *t);
    *a = (*pp)-)kdat;
    while ((*pp)-)isnode)    {
        ti = *t;
        *t = (*pp)-)faddr;
        release_node(b_fd, ti, 0);
        *pp = (struct b_node *) get_node(b_fd, *t);
        *a = (*pp)-)kdat;
    }
    return (*pp)-)faddr;
}


/* ---- Delete the key x with addr ad from the b-tree opened as file b_fd -- */
int delete_key(tree, x, ad)
int tree;
char *x;
ADDR ad;
{
    struct b_node *pp, *qp, *yp, *zp;
    int rt_len, J, comb;
    ADDR p, adr, q, *b, q1, y, z;
    ADDR get_addr(), next_key();
    register struct b_hdr *hp;
    char *a;

    if (tree )= MAXNDX || fds [tree] == 0)
        return ERROR;
    b_fd = fds [tree];
    hp = (struct b_hdr *) get_node(b_fd, (ADDR) 1);
    p = hp-)root;

/* ----------- First, locate the key, address to delete ------------- */
    if (!p) {
        release_node(b_fd, (ADDR) 1, 0);
        return OK;
    }
```

Listing A-17 (continued)

```c
        pp = (struct b_node *) get_node(b_fd, p);
        if (!search_tree (&p, &pp, hp, x, &a))  {
            release_node(b_fd, (ADDR) 1, 0);
            release_node(b_fd, p, 0);
            return OK;
        }
/* key is on file. addr must match. look at successive equal keys */
        adr = get_addr(p, &pp, hp, a);
/* the file address must be the same as called out */
        while (adr != ad)   {
            adr = next_key(&p, &pp, hp, &a);
            if (keycmp(a, x, hp->klen)) {
                release_node(b_fd, (ADDR) 1, 0);
                release_node(b_fd, p, 0);
                return OK;
            }
        }
/* ----------------- p, pp, a all point to a matching key
        Now get down to the leaf if this isn't one --------------- */
        if (pp->isnode) {
            b = (ADDR *) (a + hp->klen);
            q = *b;
            qp = (struct b_node *) get_node(b_fd, q);
            while (qp->isnode)  {
                q1 = qp->faddr;
                release_node(b_fd, q, 0);
                q = q1;
                qp = (struct b_node *) get_node(b_fd, q);
            }
/* Move the left-most key from the leaf to where the deleted key is */

            movmem(qp->kdat, a, hp->klen);
            release_node(b_fd, p, 1);
            p = q;
            a = qp->kdat;
            b = (ADDR *) (a + hp->klen);
            qp->faddr = *b;
            pp = qp;
        }
        b_nbr [tree] = p;
        k_ptr [tree] = (a - pp->kdat) / (hp->klen + sizeof(ADDR));

/* -------------------Delete the key from the leaf ----------------------*/
        rt_len = (pp->kdat + ((hp->m - 1) * (hp->klen + sizeof(ADDR)))) - a;
        movmem(a + (hp->klen + sizeof(ADDR)), a, rt_len);
        setmem(a + rt_len, hp->klen + sizeof(ADDR), '\0');
        pp->nkeys--;
        if (k_ptr [tree] > pp->nkeys)   {
            if (pp->r_bro) {
                b_nbr [tree] = pp->r_bro;
                k_ptr [tree] = 0;
```

Listing A-17 (continued)

```
        }
        else
            k_ptr [tree]--;
    }
/* ------If the node is under-populated, adjust for that ----------------- */
    while (pp-)nkeys (= (hp-)m - 1) / 2 && p != hp-)root){
        comb = FALSE;
        z = pp-)bu.prnt;
        if (pp-)r_bro)  {       /* if there is a right sibling, */
            y = pp-)r_bro;
            yp = (struct b_node *) get_node(b_fd, y);
            if (yp-)nkeys + pp-)nkeys ( hp-)m-1 && yp-)bu.prnt == z){
                comb = TRUE;
                combine_nodes(tree, pp, yp, hp);
            }
            else
                release_node(b_fd, y, 0);
        }
        if (!comb && pp-)l_bro) {   /* if there is a left sibling, */
            y = pp-)l_bro;
            yp = (struct b_node *) get_node(b_fd, y);
            if (yp-)bu.prnt == z)   { /* only combine/distribute siblings */
                if (yp-)nkeys + pp-)nkeys ( hp-)m-1) {
                    comb = TRUE;
                    combine_nodes(tree, yp, pp, hp);
                }
                else    {
                    even_dist(tree, yp, pp, hp);/* redistribute keys between */
                    release_node(b_fd, p, 1);   /* this node & left */
                    release_node(b_fd, y, 1);
                    release_node(b_fd, (ADDR) 1, 0);
                    return OK;
                }
            }
        }
        if (!comb)  {       /* have neither combined nor distributed w/left */

            y = pp-)r_bro;
            yp = (struct b_node *) get_node(b_fd, y);
            even_dist(tree, pp, yp, hp);        /* redistribute keys between */
            release_node(b_fd, y, 1);           /* this node & right */
            release_node(b_fd, p, 1);
            release_node(b_fd, (ADDR) 1, 0);
            return OK;
        }
/* --- if we got here, two child nodes were combined and a key was,
        therefore, deleted from a parent node ----- */
        p = z;
        pp = (struct b_node *) get_node(b_fd, p);
    }
```

Listing A-17 (continued)

```
    if (!pp->nkeys)                      /* if the root node became empty */{
        hp->root = pp->faddr;            /* left child becomes root */
        pp->isnode = 0;
        pp->faddr = 0;
        pp->bu.dlptr = hp->nxt_free;     /* point to next available */
        hp->nxt_free = p;                /* point header here */
    }
    if (!hp->root)                       /* if the tree became empty */
        hp->rmost = hp->lmost = 0;
    release_node(b_fd, p, 1);
    release_node(b_fd, (ADDR) 1, 1);
    return OK;
}


/* ------------ Combine the contents of two sibling nodes. ------------ */
static VOID combine_nodes(tree, left, right, hp)
int tree;
struct b_node *left, *right;
struct b_hdr *hp;
{
    ADDR lf, rt, p;
    int rt_len, lf_len;
    register char *a;
    register ADDR *b;
    struct b_node *par;
    ADDR c;
    char *j;

    lf = right->l_bro;
    rt = left->r_bro;
/* ---- find the parent of these siblings ---- */
    p = left->bu.prnt;
    parent(lf, p, &par, &j, hp);
/* --- move key from parent to end of left sibling --- */
    lf_len = left->nkeys * (hp->klen + sizeof(ADDR));
    a = left->kdat + lf_len;
    movmem(j, a, hp->klen);
    setmem(j, hp->klen + sizeof(ADDR), '\0');
/* --- move keys from right sibling to left --- */
    b = (ADDR *) (a + hp->klen);
    *b = right->faddr;
    rt_len = right->nkeys * (hp->klen + sizeof(ADDR));
    a = (char *) (b + 1);
    movmem(right->kdat, a, rt_len);
/* --- point lower nodes to their new parent --- */
    if (left->isnode)
        reparent(b, right->nkeys + 1, lf, hp);
/* --- if global key pointers -> to the right sibling, change to -> left --- */
    if (b_nbr [tree] == left->r_bro)     {
```

Listing A-17 (continued)

```
        b_nbr [tree] = right->l_bro;
        k_ptr [tree] += left->nkeys + 1;
    }
/* --- update control values in left sibling node --- */
    left->nkeys += right->nkeys + 1;    /* # keys*/
    c = hp->nxt_free;                    /* return right node to system */
    hp->nxt_free = left->r_bro;
    if (hp->rmost == left->r_bro)        /* change right-most node if appr */
        hp->rmost = right->l_bro;
    left->r_bro = right->r_bro;          /* connect to right sibling */
    setmem(right, NODELEN, '\0');
    right->bu.dlptr = c;
/* --- point the deleted node's right brother to this left brother --- */
    if (left->r_bro)    {
        right = (struct b_node *) get_node(b_fd, left->r_bro);
        right->l_bro = lf;
        release_node(b_fd, left->r_bro, 1);
    }
/* --- remove key from parent node --- */

    par->nkeys--;
    if (!par->nkeys)
        left->bu.prnt = 0;
    else    {
        rt_len = par->kdat + (par->nkeys *
                (hp->klen + sizeof(ADDR))) - j;
        movmem(j + hp->klen + sizeof(ADDR), j, rt_len);
    }
    release_node(b_fd, lf, 1);
    release_node(b_fd, rt, 1);
    release_node(b_fd, p, 1);


    }


/* -------------- Insert key x and record address ad into b-tree ---------- */

int insert_key(tree, x, ad, unique)
int tree;
char *x;
ADDR ad;
int unique;
{
    struct b_hdr *hp;
    char k [MXKEY + 1], *a;
    struct b_node *pp, *yp;
    struct b_node *bp;
    int nl_flag, rt_len, i, j;
    ADDR t, p, sv;
    ADDR find_leaf(), new_bnode();
    register ADDR *b;
```

Listing A-17 (continued)

```
    int left_shift, right_shift;

    if (tree )= MAXNDX || fds [tree] == 0)
        return ERROR;
    b_fd = fds [tree];
    hp = (struct b_hdr *) get_node(b_fd,(ADDR) 1);
    p = 0;
    sv = 0;
    nl_flag = 0;
    movmem(x, k, hp->klen);
    t = hp->root;
/* ------------ Find the place in the tree to make the insertion ------- */
    if (t) {
        pp = (struct b_node *) get_node(b_fd, t);
        if (search_tree(&t, &pp, hp, k, &a))    {
            if (unique) {
                release_node(b_fd, t, 0);
                release_node(b_fd, 1, 0);
                return ERROR;
            }
            else  {
                find_leaf(&t, &pp, hp, &a, &j);
                k_ptr [tree] = j;
            }
        }
        else
            k_ptr [tree] = ((a - pp->kdat) /
                    (hp->klen + sizeof(ADDR))) + 1;
        b_nbr [tree] = t;
    }
/* --------- Insert the new key into the leaf node ------------- */
    while (t)  {
        nl_flag = 1;
        rt_len = (pp->kdat + ((hp->m - 1) *
                (hp->klen + sizeof(ADDR)))) - a;
        movmem(a, a + hp->klen + sizeof(ADDR), rt_len);
        movmem(k, a, hp->klen);
        b = (ADDR *) (a + hp->klen);
        *b = ad;

        if (!pp->isnode)   {
            b_nbr [tree] = t;
            k_ptr [tree] = ((a - pp->kdat) /
                    (hp->klen + sizeof(ADDR))) + 1;
        }
        pp->nkeys++;
        if (pp->nkeys ( hp->m) {
            release_node(b_fd, t, 1);
            release_node(b_fd, (ADDR) 1, 1);
            return OK;
        }
```

Listing A-17 (continued)

```
/* -----------Redistribute the keys across two sibling nodes  -----------*/
        left_shift = 0;
        right_shift = 0;
        if (pp->l_bro)  {
            yp = (struct b_node *) get_node(b_fd, pp->l_bro);
            if (yp->nkeys < hp->m - 1 && yp->bu.prnt == pp->bu.prnt){
                left_shift = 1;
                even_dist(tree, yp, pp, hp);
            }
            release_node(b_fd, pp->l_bro, left_shift);
        }
        if (!left_shift && pp->r_bro)   {
            yp = (struct b_node *) get_node(b_fd, pp->r_bro);
            if (yp->nkeys < hp->m - 1 && yp->bu.prnt == pp->bu.prnt){
                right_shift = 1;
                even_dist(tree, pp, yp, hp);
            }
            release_node(b_fd, pp->r_bro, right_shift);
        }
        if (left_shift || right_shift)  {
            release_node(b_fd, t, 1);
            release_node(b_fd, (ADDR) 1, 1);
            return OK;
        }
        p = new_bnode(hp);
/* --------------- Split the node into two nodes ------------------- */
        if ((bp = (struct b_node *) malloc(NODELEN)) == 0)
            fatal(9);
        setmem(bp, NODELEN, '\0');
        pp->nkeys = hp->m / 2;
        b = (ADDR *) (pp->kdat + (((hp->m / 2) + 1) *
            (hp->klen + sizeof(ADDR))) - sizeof(ADDR));
        bp->faddr = *b;
        bp->nkeys = hp->m - ((hp->m / 2) + 1);
        rt_len = (((hp->m + 1) / 2) - 1) *
                (hp->klen + sizeof(ADDR));
        a = (char *) (b + 1);
        movmem(a, bp->kdat, rt_len);
        bp->r_bro = pp->r_bro;
        pp->r_bro = p;
        bp->l_bro = t;
        bp->isnode = pp->isnode;
        a -= hp->klen + sizeof(ADDR);
        movmem(a, k, hp->klen);
        setmem(a, rt_len + hp->klen + sizeof(ADDR), '\0');

        if (hp->rmost == t)
            hp->rmost = p;
        if (t == b_nbr [tree] && k_ptr [tree] > pp->nkeys){
            b_nbr [tree] = p;
            k_ptr [tree] -= pp->nkeys + 1;
```

```
        }
        ad = p;
        sv = t;
        t = pp->bu.prnt;
        if (t)
            bp->bu.prnt = t;
        else    {
            p = new_bnode(hp);
            pp->bu.prnt = p;
            bp->bu.prnt = p;
        }
        put_node(b_fd, ad, bp);
/* ---- If the pre-split node had a right brother, that node must now
   point to the new node as its left brother ------------------- */
        if (bp->r_bro) {
            yp = (struct b_node *) get_node(b_fd, bp->r_bro);
            yp->l_bro = ad;
            release_node(b_fd, bp->r_bro, 1);
        }
/* ---- If this is not a leaf, point the children to this parent --- */
        if (bp->isnode)
            reparent(&bp->faddr, bp->nkeys + 1, ad, hp);
        release_node(b_fd, sv, 1);
        if (t) {
            pp = (struct b_node *) get_node(b_fd, t);
            a = pp->kdat;
            b = &pp->faddr;
            while (*b != bp->l_bro) {
                a += hp->klen + sizeof(ADDR);
                b = (ADDR *) (a - sizeof(ADDR));
            }
        }
        free(bp);
    }
/* -------------------- Create a new root --------------------- */
    if (!p)
        p = new_bnode(hp);
    if ((bp = (struct b_node *) malloc(NODELEN)) == 0)
        fatal(9);
    setmem(bp, NODELEN, '\0');
    bp->isnode = nl_flag;
    bp->bu.prnt = 0;
    bp->r_bro = 0;
    bp->l_bro = 0;
    bp->nkeys = 1;
    bp->faddr = sv;
    a = bp->kdat + hp->klen;
    b = (ADDR *) a;
    *b = ad;
    movmem(k, bp->kdat, hp->klen);
    put_node(b_fd, p, bp);
```

Listing A-17 (continued)

```
    free(bp);
    hp->root = p;
    if (!nl_flag)   {
        hp->rmost = p;
        hp->lmost = p;
        b_nbr [tree] = p;
        k_ptr [tree] = 1;
    }
    release_node(b_fd, (ADDR) 1, 1);
    return OK;
}


/* ----- Evenly distribute the contents of two adjacent sibling nodes ------ */
static VOID even_dist(tree, left, right, hp)
int tree;
struct b_node *left, *right;
struct b_hdr *hp;
{
    int n1, n2, no_keys, len;
    ADDR *b, r, z;
    char *c, *d, *e;
    struct b_node *zp;

    n1 = (left->nkeys + right->nkeys) / 2;      /* # keys for left */
    if (n1 == left->nkeys)
        return;
    n2 = (left->nkeys + right->nkeys) - n1;     /* # keys for right */
    z = left->bu.prnt;
    parent(right->l_bro, z, &zp, &c, hp);
    if (left->nkeys < right->nkeys) {                  /* shift into bro w/ fewest keys */
        d = left->kdat + (left->nkeys * (hp->klen + sizeof(ADDR)));
        movmem(c, d, hp->klen);                   /* move key from parent-left*/
        d += hp->klen;
        e = right->kdat - sizeof(ADDR);
        len = ((right->nkeys - n2 - 1) *
            (hp->klen + sizeof(ADDR))) + sizeof(ADDR);
        movmem(e, d, len);                        /* from right to left  */
        if (!left->isnode)
            reparent(d, right->nkeys - n2, right->l_bro, hp);
                                                  /* assign new parent */
        e += len;                                 /* key to move to parent */
        movmem(e, c, hp->klen);                /* mv key fr rt to parent */
        e += hp->klen;                            /* data in rt to shift */
        d = right->kdat - sizeof(ADDR);           /* place in rt to shift to */
        len = (n2 * (hp->klen + sizeof(ADDR))) + sizeof(ADDR);
        movmem(e, d, len);
        setmem(d + len, e - d, '\0');
        if (!right->isnode && left->r_bro == b_nbr [tree])
            if (k_ptr [tree] < right->nkeys - n2){
```

Listing A-17 (continued)

```
                b_nbr [tree] = right->l_bro;
                k_ptr [tree] += n1 + 1;
            }
            else
                k_ptr [tree] -= right->nkeys - n2;

        }
    else  {                                    /* from left to right  */
        e = right->kdat + ((n2 - right->nkeys) *
            (hp->klen + sizeof(ADDR))) - sizeof(ADDR);
        movmem(right->kdat - sizeof(ADDR), e, (right->nkeys *
            (hp->klen + sizeof(ADDR))) + sizeof(ADDR));
        e -= hp->klen;                         /* addr for key fr parent */
        movmem(c, e, hp->klen);                 /* move key from parent  */
        d = left->kdat + (n1 * (hp->klen + sizeof(ADDR)));
        movmem(d, c, hp->klen);                 /* move key to parent  */
        setmem(d, hp->klen, '\0');


        d += hp->klen;                          /* data fr left to right */
        len = ((left->nkeys - n1 - 1) *
            (hp->klen + sizeof(ADDR))) + sizeof(ADDR);
        movmem(d, right->kdat - sizeof(ADDR), len);
        setmem(d, len, '\0');
        if (right->isnode)
            reparent(right->kdat - sizeof(ADDR),
                        left->nkeys - n1, left->r_bro, hp);
        if (!left->isnode)
            if (right->l_bro == b_nbr [tree] &&
                        k_ptr [tree] ) n1)  {
                b_nbr [tree] = left->r_bro;
                k_ptr [tree] -= n1 + 1;
            }
            else if (left->r_bro == b_nbr [tree])
                k_ptr [tree] += left->nkeys - n1;
    }
    right->nkeys = n2;
    left ->nkeys = n1;
    release_node(b_fd, z, 1);
}


/* ----- assign new parents to lower nodes where there has been a
    redistribution among the keys in two parents ------ */

static reparent(ad, kct, newp, hp)
ADDR *ad;       /* -> 1st of kct node pointers */
int kct;        /* number of node pointers shifted */
ADDR newp;      /* the new parent node  */
```

Listing A-17 (continued)

```
struct b_hdr *hp;
{
    char *cp;
    struct b_node *tmp;

    while (kct--)   {
        tmp = (struct b_node *) get_node(b_fd, *ad);
        tmp->bu.prnt = newp;
        release_node(b_fd, *ad, 1);
        cp = (char *) ad;
        cp += hp->klen + sizeof(ADDR);
        ad = (ADDR *) cp;
    }
}


/* -----compute next node address for a new node. Reuse deleted space -----*/

static ADDR new_bnode(hp)
struct b_hdr *hp;
{
    ADDR p;
    register struct b_node *pp;

    if (hp->nxt_free)   {
        p = hp->nxt_free;
        pp = (struct b_node *) get_node(b_fd, p);
        hp->nxt_free = pp->bu.dlptr;
        release_node(b_fd, p, 0);
    }
    else
        p = hp->nxt_avail++;
    return p;
}


/* ----- get the next sequential key file address starting from the global
   pointers.  update the globals. ------- */

ADDR get_next(tree)
int tree;
{
    register struct b_node *pp;
    register struct b_hdr *hp;
    ADDR *a, b, f;

    b_fd = fds [tree];
    b = b_nbr [tree];
    if (!b)
        return find_first(tree);
```

```
        pp = (struct b_node *) get_node(b_fd, b);
        hp = (struct b_hdr *) get_node(b_fd, (ADDR) 1);
        if (k_ptr [tree] == pp->nkeys)   {
            if (!pp->r_bro) {
                release_node(b_fd, b, 0);
                release_node(b_fd, (ADDR) 1, 0);
                return (ADDR) NULL;
            }
            b_nbr [tree] = pp->r_bro;
            k_ptr [tree] = 0;
            release_node(b_fd, b, 0);
            b = b_nbr [tree];
            pp = (struct b_node *) get_node(b_fd, b);
        }
        else
            k_ptr [tree]++;
        a = (ADDR *) (pp->kdat + (k_ptr [tree] *
                (hp->klen + sizeof(ADDR))) - sizeof(ADDR));
        f = *a;
        release_node(b_fd, b, 0);
        release_node(b_fd, (ADDR) 1, 0);
        return f;
}


/* get the previous sequential key file address starting from the global
   pointers.  update the globals. */

ADDR get_prev(tree)
int tree;
{
    register struct b_node *pp;
    register struct b_hdr *hp;
    ADDR *a, b, f;

    b_fd = fds [tree];
    b = b_nbr [tree];
    if (!b)
        return find_last(tree);
    pp = (struct b_node *) get_node(b_fd, b);
    hp = (struct b_hdr *) get_node(b_fd, (ADDR) 1);
    if (!k_ptr [tree])   {
        if (!pp->l_bro) {
            release_node(b_fd, b, 0);
            release_node(b_fd, (ADDR) 1, 0);
            return (ADDR) NULL;
        }
        b_nbr [tree] = pp->l_bro;
        release_node(b_fd, b, 0);
        b = b_nbr [tree];
        pp = (struct b_node *) get_node(b_fd, b);
        k_ptr [tree] = pp->nkeys;
```

Listing A-17 (continued)

```
    }
    else
        k_ptr [tree]--;
    a = (ADDR *) (pp->)kdat + (k_ptr [tree] *
        (hp->klen + sizeof(ADDR))) - sizeof(ADDR));
    f = *a;
    release_node(b_fd, b, 0);
    release_node(b_fd, (ADDR) 1, 0);
    return f;
}


/* ------------- find the first key in the b tree ------------- */

ADDR find_first(tree)
int tree;
{
    ADDR b, *c, p;
    register struct b_node *pp;
    register struct b_hdr *hp;

    b_fd = fds [tree];
    hp = (struct b_hdr *) get_node(b_fd, (ADDR) 1);
    p = hp->lmost;
    if (!p) {
        release_node(b_fd, (ADDR) 1, 0);
        return (ADDR) NULL;
    }
    pp = (struct b_node *) get_node(b_fd, p);
    c = (ADDR *) (pp->kdat + hp->klen);
    b = *c;
    b_nbr [tree] = p;
    k_ptr [tree] = 1;
    release_node(b_fd, p, 0);
    release_node(b_fd, (ADDR) 1, 0);
    return b;
}

/* ------------- find the last key in the b tree ---------------- */

ADDR find_last(tree)
int tree;
{
    ADDR b, *c, p;
    register struct b_node *pp;
    register struct b_hdr *hp;

    b_fd = fds [tree];
    hp = (struct b_hdr *) get_node(b_fd, (ADDR) 1);
    p = hp->rmost;
    if (!p) {
```

Listing A-17 (continued)

```
        release_node(b_fd, (ADDR) 1, 0);
        return (ADDR) NULL;
    }
    pp = (struct b_node *) get_node(b_fd, p);
    c = (ADDR *) (pp->kdat + (pp->nkeys *
            (hp->klen + sizeof(ADDR))) - sizeof(ADDR));
    b = *c;
    b_nbr [tree] = p;
    k_ptr [tree] = pp->nkeys;
    release_node(b_fd, p, 0);
    release_node(b_fd, (ADDR) 1, 0);
    return b;
}


/* ---- get the next sequential key in a tree starting from where pointers now
    point. update the pointers to the next one and return the file address -- */

static ADDR next_key(p, pp, hp, a)
ADDR *p;
struct b_node **pp;
struct b_hdr *hp;
char **a;
{
    ADDR get_addr();
    ADDR cn;
    register ADDR *b;

    if ((*pp)->isnode) {
        cn = *p;
        b = (ADDR *) (*a + hp->klen);
        *p = *b;
        release_node(b_fd, cn, 0);
        *pp = (struct b_node *) get_node(b_fd, *p);
        while ((*pp)->isnode) {
            cn = *p;
            *p = (*pp)->faddr;
            release_node(b_fd, cn, 0);
            *pp = (struct b_node *) get_node(b_fd, *p);
        }
        *a = (*pp)->kdat;
        b = (ADDR *) (*a + hp->klen);
        return *b;
    }
    *a += hp->klen + sizeof(ADDR);
    while (-1) {
        if (((*pp)->kdat + ((*pp)->nkeys)
                * (hp->klen + sizeof(ADDR))) != *a)
            return get_addr(*p, pp, hp, *a);
        if (!(*pp)->bu.prnt || !(*pp)->r_bro)
            return (ADDR) NULL;
```

Listing A-17 (continued)

```
        cn = *p;
        *p = (*pp)-)bu.prnt;
        release_node(b_fd, cn, 0);
        *pp = (struct b_node *) get_node(b_fd, *p);
        *a = (*pp)-)kdat;
        b = (ADDR *) (*a - sizeof(ADDR));
        while (*b != cn)    {
            *a += hp-)klen + sizeof(ADDR);
            b = (ADDR *) (*a - sizeof(ADDR));
        }
    }
}


/* ------ search parent, return pointer to node in par,
    pointer to ancestor key within node in c.   The node is in use
    when the function returns --- */

static parent(left, parent, pp, c, hp)
ADDR left;                 /* node # of left sibling */
ADDR parent;                  /* node # of parent */
struct b_node **pp;        /* to return pointer to parent */
char **c;                  /* to return pointer to ancestral key */
struct b_hdr *hp;
{
    ADDR *b;

    *pp = (struct b_node *) get_node(b_fd, parent);
    *c = (*pp)-)kdat;
    b = (ADDR *) (*c - sizeof(ADDR));
    while (*b != left)  {
        *c += hp-)klen + sizeof(ADDR);
        b = (ADDR *) (*c - sizeof(ADDR));
    }
}

/* ---- return the current key value to the caller's space --- */

/* This is useful for passing through the tree sequentially without
    making a file access to retrieve the key value.  Can be used in
    creating histograms or multiple-key file query hit lists */

currkey(tree, ky)
int tree;
char *ky;        /* -) caller's key string space. Current key is put here */
{
    struct b_node *pp;
    struct b_hdr *hp;
    ADDR b, p, *a;
    char *k;
    int i;
```

```c
    b_fd = fds [tree];
    b = b_nbr [tree];
    if (b)  {
        hp = (struct b_hdr *) get_node(b_fd, (ADDR) 1);
        pp = (struct b_node *) get_node(b_fd, b);
        i = k_ptr [tree];
        k = pp->kdat + ((i - 1) * (hp->klen + sizeof(ADDR)));
        while (i == 0)  {
            p = b;
            b = pp->bu.prnt;
            release_node(b_fd, p, 0);
            pp = (struct b_node *) get_node(b_fd, b);
            for (; i <= pp->nkeys; i++) {
                k = pp->kdat + ((i - 1) * (hp->klen + sizeof(ADDR)));
                a = (ADDR *) (k + hp->klen);
                if (*a == p)
                    break;
            }

        }
        movmem(k, ky, hp->klen);
        release_node(b_fd, b, 0);
        release_node(b_fd, (ADDR) 1, 0);
    }
}


/* --- get the current key -> by the globals based upon the most
   recent B-tree action.  This is useful when find_key has returned
   FALSE and you want to pick up with the next highest record, whatever
   its key value. Return the file address. ---- */

ADDR get_curr(tree)
int tree;
{
    struct b_node *pp;
    struct b_hdr *hp;
    ADDR *a, b, f = (ADDR) NULL, q;

    b_fd = fds [tree];
    b = b_nbr [tree];
    if (b)  {
        pp = (struct b_node *) get_node(b_fd, b);
        hp = (struct b_hdr *) get_node(b_fd, (ADDR) 1);
        a = (ADDR *) (pp->kdat + (k_ptr [tree] *
            (hp->klen + sizeof (ADDR))) - sizeof (ADDR));
        f = *a;
        release_node(b_fd, b, 0);
        release_node(b_fd, (ADDR) 1, 0);
    }
    return f;
}
```

```
/* ---------------------- unlock.c ------------------------- */

#include <stdio.h>
#include <fcntl.h>
#include "toolset.h"
#include "btree.h"

main (argc, argv)
int argc;
char *argv [];
{
    struct b_hdr r;
    int fd;

    if (argc < 2)   {
        printf ("\nIndex name required");
        exit ();
    }
    if ((fd = open (argv [1], O_RDWR)) == ERROR){
        printf ("\nNo index named %s can be found",argv [1]);
        exit ();
    }
    read (fd, &r, sizeof (r));
    r.in_use = 0;
    lseek (fd, 0L, 0);
    write (fd, &r, sizeof (r));
    close (fd);
}
```

Listing A-18.

A Study in Portability

How portable is the software in Appendix A? This software avoids the use of any nonstandard functions offered by the compilers. It uses **typedef** and **sizeof** wherever portability is a consideration. Finally, it uses global defines instead of constants wherever sizing could be changed to alter performance on different machines. But, the true measure of portability is not in our good intentions; it is reflected in the experiences of moving software around.

The first collection of these tools was developed on an old IMSAI 8080 computer with the BDS C compiler, a fine product. It is a respectable subset of the language, and it out-performs any of its competition. It is reliable, a bargain, and well supported. I still use it for the development of small 8080 and Z80 systems where development time is important. You can get more code working faster by using BDS C than any other way I know. It was my introduction to the C language, and the creator of the compiler, Leor Zolman, must have used up a lot of his patience sending out those postcards with answers to my stupid questions. Some day those cards are going to be collector's items. I wonder how many other people kept them.

The next version of the code was converted to the full C language when the Aztec C II compiler for CP/M began getting some respect from the reviewers. I used a desk-top Z80 computer, called the Micro Decision. The code went through two versions of Aztec C II and now works reliably with V1.06D.

(In the interim, there have been several variations of different pieces of the code implemented into various environments with various terminals. There is even one version running on a multi-user TurboDos system.)

The latest version runs on the IBM PC with MS-DOS and three different compilers. That version is published in this book.

There are very few source code differences between the CP/M-80 version and the newer MS-DOS versions. The Z80 version has a different copy of terminal.c. That is unavoidable, and it is also intentional. We want the software to be device-independent, and the two machines have different keyboards and screen commands. The CP/M version has smaller values for NODELEN in "toolset.h" and MXNODES in "cache.c." This is because of the smaller memory model in the Z80. The Z80 memory model provides a total of 64K for program and data. Aztec C86 and Lattice C implement several different memory models for MS-DOS computers. The small memory model provides for 64K of program and 64K of data. This model will support most applications.

The three different MS-DOS versions have common source code. They are compiled by using these compilers:

- Aztec C86 V3.20
- Lattice C V2.14
- DeSmet C V2.41

I have worked with two other MS-DOS compilers during the testing of the toolset software. The Digital Research C compiler was used early in the project. Recently, the Eco-C88 compiler has been used to compile and execute the programs.

Digital Research C showed up with a problem in the areas of pointer arithmetic and the calculation of addresses of structure arrays. The problems have been in the compiler through several versions, and the vendor acknowledges their existence, but no correction has been announced. They recommend a technique for avoiding the problem that involves restructuring of data formats to get around the problem in the compiler. The Digital Research C compiler performs poorly in the areas of compile time, code module size and execution speeds when compared with the others.

The Eco-C88 compiler was recently reduced in price to less than $50, and it is now the least expensive of the MS-DOS C compilers. Eco-C88 includes a development program called cc that will be very useful to programmers. You enter a command line that specifies all of the code modules in the executing program. Cc compiles only those programs it needs to compile and links all of the object files into an executable file. Cc compares the date and time of each source module with its corresponding object module and compiles only those programs with more recent source files. If the executable module is newer than all of the object modules, it bypasses the link, otherwise it links all the modules together. Cc is a wonderful program, and the generous people at EcoSoft provide its source code when you buy the compiler. At the time of this writing and because of the pressures of my publishing deadline, the tests of the toolset under the Eco-C88 compiler are incomplete, but preliminary results are promising.

The Eco-C88 compiler is the most rigid with respect to language rule compliance, and the DeSmet C compiler is the most lenient.

The file "toolset.h" has a global named "COMPILER" that is defined to global values AZTEC__C86, LATTICE, or CWARE depending on whether the Aztec, Lattice, or DeSmet compilers, respectively, are used. Future versions of the source code will include compile-time options for the Eco-C88 compiler. If you decide to buy the source code on diskette through the mail (see the foreword to this book for details), the Eco-C88 compiler option will be included.

There are differences in the compilers. The next few paragraphs address some of these differences and serve as an example of some of the difficulties you can encounter writing code that is supposed to be portable.

Aztec has a function named **bdos** that is used to manage direct console input and output. Lattice and DeSmet have direct console input/output functions, so we do not need a **bdos** function with them, even though Lattice has one. However, the sample program, "dattim.c" cannot be run with Lattice, because it requires the **bdos** function to set the date and time in MS-DOS, and Lattice's **bdos** does not support **bdos** function calls requiring two parameters. Likewise it is not used in the DeSmet environment because DeSmet has no **bdos** function.

Other differences have appeared. If you do character arithmetic with an integer result, the Lattice and Aztec compilers will extend the sign into the most significant byte of the result, while the DeSmet compiler will not. The DeSmet compiler allows a null statement (;) between functions. Aztec and Lattice issue error messages when this occurs.

The compilers disagree on the use of the `void` type for function returns. If a `void` function declaration is placed within the body of another function, the Aztec compiler treats it as a call of the function being declared. The Lattice compiler does not seem to like `void` function declarations at all, but if they are left out, a call to the function implicitly declares it to be of type integer. Then, when the function itself shows up with a return declaration of `void`, an error is reported. The only way around this is to define the VOID global to `int`, and thus, avoid (no pun intended) the `void` altogether. The DeSmet compiler seems to manage the `void` function type properly.

Address arithmetic provides some of the widest variations in language implementation. The Aztec and Lattice compilers do not allow the following statement:

```
cp1 += cp2;
```

where `cp1` and `cp2` are character pointers. They both correctly report an invalid pointer calculation. Aztec will allow this next statement, but Lattice will not.

```
cp1 = cp1 + cp2;
```

Once again, Lattice issues an error regarding an invalid pointer operation. DeSmet allows either form to be used. Kernighan and Ritchie are explicit about this (page 99 of "The C Programming Language"). Pointers may not be added but they may be subtracted yielding an integer result. If you code:

```
i = cp1 + cp2;
```

where i is an integer, the Aztec compiler issues a pointer to integer conversion warning, Lattice issues an invalid pointer operation error (which is correct), and DeSmet allows the operation. There is further disagreement about the following two statement forms:

```
cp1 -= cp2;
cp1 = cp1 - cp2;
```

In the strictest interpretation of K&R, both of these are illegal. Although they involve pointer subtraction (which is legal) they call for a pointer result (which is improper). In both cases Lattice issues a warning saying that the pointers do not point to the same objects. Aztec issues an illegal pointer calculation error for the first statement and a pointer to integer conversion warning (!) for the second statement. Once again, DeSmet allows either form.

All three compilers allow the following legitimate statement:

```
i = cp1 - cp2;
```

Performance Comparisons

For those interested in benchmarks, Table B-1 is a table of performance comparisons for compiling, linking, building libraries, and executing programs using the MS-DOS compilers.

Table B-1. Performance Comparisons

Activity	Aztec	Lattice	DeSmet
Development:			
Compile and assemble btree.c	1:33	1:40	:30
Build toolset library	:09	:08	:05
Link example	:11	:19	:08
Execution:			
Example.exe module size	24016	36366	34816
Sort 1000 disk records	:16	:23	:19
Display 1000 records	2:12	1:55	1:03

The timings were made by using the default options and small memory models for the compilers and linkers. I used an enhanced IBM AT equipped with a 20 Megabyte Winchester disk drive and 512K bytes of RAM with the MS-DOS 3.0 operating system.

Summary of Compilers

Table B-2 is a list of the compilers discussed in this appendix and the names and addresses of their vendors.

Table B-2. Compiler Reference List

Compiler	Processor	Operating System	Vendor
BDS C	8080/Z80	CP/M-80	BD Software P.O. Box 9 Brighton, MA 02135
Aztec C II Aztec C86	8080/Z80 8088/86	CP/M-80 MS-DOS CP/M-86	Manx Software Systems P.O. Box 55 Shrewsbury, NJ 07701
Digital Research C	8088/86	MS-DOS CP/M-86	Digital Research P.O Box 579 160 Central Avenue Pacific Grove, CA 93950
Lattice C	8088/86	MS-DOS CP/M-86	Lattice, Inc. P.O. Box 3072 Glen Ellyn, IL 60138
DeSmet C	8088/86	MS-DOS CP/M-86	C Ware Corporation P.O. Box C Sunnyvale, CA 94087
Eco-C88	8088/86	MS-DOS	Ecosoft Inc. 6413 North College Avenue Indianapolis, IN 46220

Global Definitions

Table B-3 is a summary of the global definitions that are related to the porting of the software. As you implement the software, consider each of these. detailed discussions are available throughout this book.

Table B-3. Toolset Global Definitions

Source File	Global	Use
toolset.h	COMPILER	defines which compiler is used
	NODELEN	length of logical sector
	ADDR	record address variable type
keys.h	HELP	defines the keystroke for HELP
	GO	” ” ” ” GO
	DITTO	” ” ” ” DITTO
	HT	screen character spacing for \t
screen.h	SCRNID	screen separator in template
	SCBUFF	maximum template buffer size
	MAXSCRNS	maximum templates per file
	MAXFIELDS	maximum fields per template
	FLDFILL	entry field id character
menu.h	MXSELS	maximum selections per menu
sort.h	NOFLDS	maximum sort fields
menu.c	DEPTH	depth of menu nesting
	HEIGHT	number of screen lines
	WIDTH	number of screen columns
cache.c	MXNODES	maximum cache memory nodes
files.c	MAXFILES	maximum files open at once
screen.c	PADCHAR	ASCII file padding character
btree.c	MXKEY	maximum index key length
	MAXNDX	maximum B-trees open at once
terminal.c	COLOR	TRUE = IBM color graphics card

Summary of Portability

In review, we can see that there are differences between the CP/M and MS-DOS implementations that reflect differences in the terminal and the operating system. But, aside from these, the code is portable between two different computers using two different compilers (from the same manufacturer, however).

We can also see almost 100% source code compatibility between three different compilers for the same (MS-DOS) operating system. But, it took some conscious effort to get it that way. Each time the code was ported to another compiler, it became more portable, because we made sure that any modifications would be acceptable to the earlier compilers. This way, the code becomes a common style of C language programming, and we get better at writing portable code, because we become more sensitive to portability issues.

Index